A *word about this series from* Toastmasters International

Who needs another book on public speaking, let alone a series of them? After all, this is a skill best learned by practice and "just doing it," you say.

But if practice is the best solution to public speaking excellence, why is this world so full of speakers who can't speak effectively? Consider politicians, business executives, sales professionals, teachers, trainers, clerics, and even "professional" speakers who often fail to reach their audiences because they make elementary mistakes, such as speaking too fast or too long, failing to prepare adequately, and forgetting to consider their audiences.

As we experience in Toastmasters Clubs, practice and feedback are important and play major roles in developing your speaking skills. But insight and tips from people who have already been where you are might help ease some bumps along the road, reinforce some basic public speaking techniques, and provide guidance on handling special speech problems and situations you may encounter. The purpose of *The Essence of Public Speaking Series* is to help you prepare for the unexpected, warn you of the pitfalls, and help you ensure that the message you want to give is indeed the same one the audience hears.

This series features the accumulated wisdom of experts in various speech-related fields. The books are written by trained professionals who have spent decades writing and delivering speeches and training others. The series covers the spectrum of speaking, including writing, using humor, customizing particular topics for various audiences, and incorporating technology into presentations.

Whether you are an inexperienced or seasoned public speaker, *The Essence of Public Speaking Series* belongs on your bookshelf because no matter how good you are, there is always room for improvement. The books are your key to becoming a more effective speaker. Do you have the self-discipline to put into practice the techni~~~~ ~~ ~~~~~ offered in them?

D0189951

I honestly believe that every person who truly wants to become a confident and eloquent public speaker can become one. Success or failure depends on attitude. There is no such thing as a "hopeless case." If you want to enhance your personal and professional progress, I urge you to become a better public speaker by doing two things:

- Read these books.
- Get on your feet and practice what you've learned.

Terrence J. McCann
Executive Director, Toastmasters International

"Motivating Your Audience: Speaking from the Heart *provides a clear and effective format that enables the speaker to ignite the 'fires of motivation' in his listeners! It is a worthy resource for the motivational speaker.*"

— *Don Ench,* Toastmasters International

"*If you have been searching for a book that gives the essential elements of how to give a memorable motivational speech—THIS IS IT!!* Dr. McCarty breaks down a motivational speech to its core and provides simple steps for anyone to create the environment needed to present a truly inspiring speech. Learn how to touch the hearts of your audience, help them discover and sing their songs, and make a lasting impression by reading and following the ideas presented in the book."

— *Robert E. Barnhill, III,* JD, CPA/ PFS, CFP; President, L*I*V*E Speakers, Inc.; Toastmasters International Accredited Speaker and 1996–97 International President

"*If I were climbing Mt. Everest, I would want the best Sherpa guide I could find. On my climb to be the best motivational speaker I could become, I would want only one guide and he would be Hanoch McCarty. If you would like to have such a guide to the top of the motivational speaking mountain, this book deserves first place in your 'speaker's backpack.'*"

— *Sidney B. Simon,* Professor Emeritus, University of Massachusetts, speaker, trainer, educator

"*There are few speakers in the world for whom I would voluntarily travel out of my way just to hear them speak but Dr. Hanoch McCarty is one of them. He is simply that good. As I read this incredible book, I laughed and I cried. I thought about new things I had not considered before. In short, I was motivated! And you will be, too!*"

—Dr. Matthew Weinstein, author, *Playfair*

MOTIVATING YOUR AUDIENCE

Speaking from the Heart

HANOCH McCARTY

WILLIAM D. THOMPSON
Series Editor

ALLYN AND BACON

Boston   London   Toronto   Sydney   Tokyo   Singapore

**To the best motivational speaker I have ever known,
Jean Wasserman McCarty, my mother.**
Her dramatic style, her intuitive command of nonverbal cues,
and her mastery of the nuances of the English language were
informed by a loving and wise heart. I never get up to speak
without calling upon the skills she taught me by her example.

**And to the most charismatic person—
and speaker—that I've every known,
Douglas Lawrence Bendell, my brother.**
His self-confidence, infectious smile, and energetic commitment
to every project he has worked on became my definition of
"intentionality" and credibility. He has always been my mentor.

Copyright © 1999 by Allyn and Bacon
A Viacom Company
160 Gould Street
Needham Heights, MA 02294

Internet: www.abacon.com
America Online: keyword: College Online

0-205-26894-3

Printed in the United States of America
10 9 8 7 6 5 4 3 2 1   02 01 00 99 98

Contents

Acknowledgments

I would like to acknowledge the inestimable help I received from Bill Thompson, my editor, without whose patience and encouragement this book would not exist; Joanna Slan for her essential part of the beginning of this project; and my great friends and colleagues in the National Speakers Association, especially my coauthors on *A 4th Course of Chicken Soup for the Soul,* Jack Canfield and Mark Victor Hansen.

No project could have gotten more help than that I received from Meladee McCarty, my coauthor on four previous books and my best friend, best brainstormer, best source of feedback, and my life partner and sweetheart.

Dr. McCarty is eager to hear from readers of this book. He can be reached at P.O. Box 66, Galt, California 95632; (209) 745-2212.

 # INTRODUCTION

THE CHALLENGE OF MOTIVATING OTHERS

You've been asked to give a motivational speech. The thought is oddly troubling. "Who am I to motivate anyone else?" you ponder. Can anyone be motivated by anyone else? Self-doubt assails you. Sound familiar? It's probably why you're reading this book.

As you go further into this book, you'll find a discussion of motivational speeches. What are they? How do they differ from any other kind of speech? And so on. But, for now, let's just look at the idea of motivating someone else. You wonder, as you are planning your speech, "How can I motivate this group? What can I say or do that will materially affect their motivations? And just what do I want them to be motivated to do?"

After all these years of speaking in front of audiences from coast to coast, I have come to believe that *it is nearly impossible to motivate someone else.* Let's pretend that in front of you is an audience of people with no motivation of their own. They all suffer from apathy, anomie, boredom, or whatever malaise you can imagine, which either removed their own natural motivation or prevented them from developing any of their own. There they sit, immobile, impassive, uncaring. And you are to motivate them!

Daunting task, isn't it? How can I get my motivations across to them and implanted in them so they will then be "motivated?" If it sounds impossible, that's because it probably is impossible. I don't mean that the task of giving a motivational speech is impossible, I just believe that one cannot "give" motivation to someone else *unless one can tap into the motivations already present in that person!* If you could truly assemble an audience of totally unmotivated people (they'd be more likely found in an asylum!), you'd find it impossible to motivate them, because you cannot connect with the motivations that are already there.

If, on the other hand, you find yourself in front of an actively hostile audience, as difficult as it might be to motivate them positively, you at least have a reasonable chance—since they are already powerfully motivated—with their anger, upset, hostility, or whatever set of concerns or problems have left them feeling the way they do. As the speaker entering such a room, if you've done your homework—as we'll explain elsewhere in this book—you can connect with those motivations and possibly turn them around toward positive dimensions.

So the act of motivating someone else, singly or in large groups called "audiences," demands that you understand and attempt to connect with their feelings, concerns, values, experiences, and unmet needs.

ALL HUMANS ARE MOTIVATED

All humans are motivated by their unmet needs or unfulfilled wants. If you are perfectly content, you will stay where you are, doing what you are doing. It is only when you discover in yourself a need that you rise, look around, and seek the desired object. Sitting in front of your television, you are absorbed in the program. Gradually, you become aware of hunger, or thirst, or pressure in your bladder. When one of these needs becomes strong enough to overwhelm your interest in the program, you find yourself going to the refrigerator or to the bathroom. That's called *motivation*.

In order to understand motivation, let us create a scenario: You are at work. You love your job. You've been doing it for only a few years and find yourself increasing in skill and achievement. There's a fascination to every challenge in the job. You are already fully motivated, aren't you? You don't need to attend a motivational talk. In fact, it might be an annoying distraction to take you away from your work today to bring you to a motivating speaker.

Now, let's cut ahead in a time machine to five years later. You've been doing this job a long time. There don't seem to be any surprises any more. There's been a salary freeze because the company's been having hard times and tough competition from foreign factories. The lack of available funding has prevented you from instituting the new procedures you know could make a big difference in productivity. You feel frustrated. There's been a rumor of a possible takeover bid, and the company mentioned is famous for brutal personnel cuts they call "right-sizing."

All the employees in your division are asked to attend a conference. The conference begins with a motivational keynote address. Are you a candidate for motivation? I think the answer could be a resounding, "YES!" if the speaker is aware of the issues and has good, positive and reliable information to share. You are ready for motivation because, in this scenario, you may have the following motivations: *boredom* with a job done too long and too predictably—the challenge and fun have faded; *anger,* because you've not been given raises that you feel you deserve; *frustration,* because you have a picture of how to improve your work but lack of funding has blocked you; *fear,* because of possible personnel cuts. All of these feelings are motivations. Equally, you are a candidate for motivation because you have the desire for achievement, a need to reach excellence, a love for the challenge of making a sale. You're ready to be motivated, because your job at the company, no matter how difficult things have been lately, still represents to you the field you most loved and the one you studied for years to master. You remember the good times in the company and are motivated to try to bring the company back to those times. You may be ready for motivation because you are an upbeat person, one who is always ready to tackle seemingly insurmountable tasks and conquer them. You see, there are many motivations and many reasons that people become motivated.

YOU MUST UNDERSTAND YOUR AUDIENCE'S MOTIVATIONS

The speaker, to be successful, has to understand the audience's motivations, be aware of them, and speak to them directly at some point in his or her presentation. Listening to a speaker who does so, you will feel motivated. You may come up to the speaker afterward and say, "I'm so glad you came here. I really needed to hear your talk! You (reassured) (gave hope to) (entertained) me."

In that same audience are people with many different motivations. It is important to realize that not everyone is "on the same page" at the same time—motivationally. Some will be new hires, possibly motivated by their desire to seem "gung ho," energized, and attentive. Others may be new hires who are still disoriented, somewhat confused, anxious about being seen as competent, unsure as to whether they will fit in to the group or if they will succeed. There will be a group of experienced employees who are used to being seen as the top rung, the best at their jobs. Some of those will come in wanting to be seen as highly involved because it fits their idea of their image in the company. Others, similarly experienced, may want to be seen as blasé: "There's nothing new in this stuff for me; been there, done that." We could go on and on: The range of possible motivations and combinations of motivations that may exist in members of a group is nearly infinite. The important fact to remember is: Everyone is motivated by something—unless he or she is in a coma! If you can determine what the major motivations are in this audience, you can become a "motivational speaker."

MOTIVATION IS NOT A PAINT JOB

The successful motivational speaker doesn't motivate people in the sense of giving them something they didn't have— painting the motivation on their surface. Instead, he or she reaches into the audience, finds their major motivations or those most appropriate to the goals of the presentation, and taps into them, using those motivations as the core components of the presentation.

If you are fabulously wealthy and I offer you a chance to save $2.00 by bringing in a coupon to my store, it's unlikely I've motivated you to be a customer. Even with a nice coupon, beautifully printed, I haven't motivated you because your money needs—at least at that amount of money—are fully satisfied. I cannot *give you* a motivation. Picture the moment that you've just eaten and are satiated; you've pushed away from the table and announced, "I am stuffed." At that moment I offer you another steak, perfectly cooked. I am wasting my time, for your food needs are completely satisfied. To motivate you, I must find what wants or needs you still have not fulfilled.

NO ONE MOTIVATES EVERYONE ALL THE TIME!

So it *is* possible to be a motivator. You can make a difference with an audience and with many, if not most, of the individuals in that audience. But make no mistake: There will be people in any audience whom you do not and cannot reach. Even after your very best performance: You did your homework; you connected with the audience in the most powerful way possible; it was the peak moment of your career as a speaker; you received a thundering, sustained, standing ovation. There was a large crowd of thankful, delighted participants waiting to speak with you. Several had tears of gratitude in their eyes. I don't want to diminish your pleasure. After all, you've done your job. You've given that motivational talk, and it has succeeded. The program planner said you even exceeded her expectations. The warm glow of success suffuses your body.

But, even at this moment of triumph, do not fail to notice the several people who sneaked out early or who left just a few minutes before your presentation. Look around the room at those who do not choose to come up to speak with you. Some are muttering darkly, sarcastically, to their buddies. Look at those who politely waited until you are done, and in the midst of your standing ovation, left early. These were the people whom you did not reach. Let me reassure you that it's unlikely that *anyone* could have reached those few today. They came here with the intent of not being reached, of not being motivated. Frankly, it would have been a miracle if you had reached them. Every group has such people. The very best speakers and the very best speeches still leave a small, vocal bunch of people who were not satisfied, could not be satisfied.

In one presentation I did for a major corporation, there were over 2,000 people in the room. I had spent weeks researching the group and its needs. I had flown in a month earlier and interviewed 16 key people in order to focus my talk exactly to the group, its history, and its needs. To my great delight, they bestowed a true standing ovation on me. The meeting planner told me that he counted at least 150 people waiting to talk with me after it was all over. I received the highest ratings of any speaker in the meeting planner's eight years with the company. Yet, in those same rating sheets were 15 people who rated it "one of the least interesting sessions" and one who complained bitterly about the quality of the seating in the room and the lack of good circulating air conditioning!

Here is the mystery: You did reach some of those people who couldn't be reached by the last speaker. In that previous presentation, they walked out even more convinced that things are bad, the job stinks, the new program will fail, or, simply, they were contrary to the message of the day. Today, you surprise them by reaching them. You somehow tapped into their motivations, evaded their defenses, broke through, and got them to believe again. And the ones you failed to reach? Maybe next time. Or maybe the next speaker. Or maybe not. Some people are so negative, so burnt out, so convinced of the rightness of their refusal to participate, that they cannot be reached by anyone at any time. Others are just not ready to be reached today. In a sense, they aren't ripe for motivation now. At some later date, who can say? The fact that there was that irreducible minimum of unreachables at your talk is not a sign of your failure. It is simply a fact of human groups.

I had the great privilege some years ago to share the platform at a national conference in Atlanta, Georgia, with the late world-renowned psychologist and author, Carl Rogers. We were on a panel together. I confess that I was so awestruck by this man, whose writings had been a central part of my own training, that my contributions to the discussion were very limited indeed. At one point in the evening,

Dr. Rogers was asked about how his fame had affected his ability to do his work with people effectively. He indicated that it was a continuing problem to have to deal with people putting him on a pedestal and elevating even his most mundane remark into a kind of revealed truth. Nevertheless, he said, it was also seductive to be treated that way, and he constantly struggled to restore himself, in people's eyes, to a common, equal, human perspective without buying in to the level of expertise and magical qualities with which they would try to invest him.

In this context, he told a story. He said that he had been teaching at a well-known conference and training center on the West Coast in a beautiful room with a whole wall of picture windows facing the ocean. There were over a hundred therapists, psychologists, and other professionals there attending his workshop for the week. He sat on a chair, but most participants sat on the carpeting at his feet. As he was speaking about some psychological insight or other, the room was rapt with attention. Suddenly, one of the participants called out, "Look! A rainbow!" Just like children, the whole group leaped to their feet and ran to the windows to enjoy the sight, leaving Dr. Rogers sitting alone facing the empty spots where his audience had just been! He confessed that he was put out by this and then realized that he was not as free of playing "guru" as he had thought. He, too, got up and went to see the rainbow. While standing at the window, listening to the oohs and ahhs uttered by many, the man standing nearest to him muttered under his breath, "Awww, this is nothing! This isn't half as nice as the rainbow I saw last month in Hawaii!"

Dr. Rogers smiled as he told this story. *"You see,"* he explained, *"for this man, even God Himself gets a 'C-minus' in rainbow making!* There are people out there who cannot be pleased by anyone or anything!"

If you can keep the number of people who cannot be pleased down to 1 or 2 percent of those attending, you are doing a spectacular job. It is just not a reasonable expectation to think you'll ever get to 100 percent of your audience. Keep in mind that the motivational business involves a partnership between you, the speaker or "motivator," and each audience member, each of whom brings his or her own motivations, strong or weak, positive or negative, ready or unready, to the conference room. It is at that moment that you have the opportunity to become a motivational speaker—when you involve yourself in a relationship with your audience. You will cooperate with them. As you will see, they want motivation, and you want to be motivating. The trick is going to be whether or not you learn to connect yourself, your words, your ideas to their need, their background and experiences, their ways of seeing the world. Make that connection, and you will be well on your way to being an excellent motivational speaker.

All speakers use words, gestures, movement, stories, ideas, facts, and techniques to reach their audiences. You will mold all these elements into a speech and deliver it, and, if you speak to the heart of each member of the audience, to the heart and not just to the mind, you have reached your goal. You cannot simply "convince" your audience, by force of reason, by weight of facts and figures, to become motivated in some direction. Ideas and facts alone do not motivate well. Some years ago a study was conducted on people's values. The researchers, in order to discover what people valued the most, asked large groups to list what they thought they would save if they arrived at their homes only to discover their homes were on fire. Group after group was asked to list the first ten items they'd try to rescue from the fire. The lists made enormous sense. People saved their families, their valuables, and their irreplaceable keepsakes. Some time later, another researcher, interested in "panic behavior," looked at what people actually *did* save when confronted with a house fire. The lists were considerably less sensible. Several examples are worth noting: A woman saved a picture of her cat and left the cat; a man saved a receipt for $10,000 and left the money; another saved a written description of his valuable antique violin and left the instrument. When people are calm and rational their behavior is much different from those moments when they are emotional and feeling. Similarly, we are taught to believe that we are motivated by reason, yet many studies have shown that people's rationales for their behavior may sound logical but are often created *ex post facto* to explain otherwise irrational choices. In short, we behave more out of our hearts than from cold logic. If you would motivate others you must become attuned to what touches the heart.

I was a high school teacher working at an inner-city high school in an economically depressed area of New York City. A big, old, shabby building, crammed with many more students than it was designed for, it was beset with gang violence and suffered from an often dispirited faculty. I had taught there only about a year when I came down with pneumonia and had to stay home for about two weeks. When I returned, I entered the office to pick up my mail. As I went through the mail in my box, I felt an arm around my shoulders. It was my principal, Paul Balser. I did not know him well. There were over 185 teachers in the building and perhaps 3,500 students. I thought he didn't know me at all. I was surprised at his familiarity. He said, "We missed you. Glad you're back." "You missed me?" I replied incredulously, "What do you mean by that? You had a substitute." Mr. Balser smiled, "Oh, we had someone who covered your classes, but we couldn't find anyone who could fill your shoes!" I didn't even know that he knew anything about me, but there he was telling me that I had something of value to share with kids in his building, that I was *irreplaceable*. After that, I would have done almost anything for that man! Talk about motivation! Mr. Balser spoke to the heart. All of us crave being valuable, making a significant contribution. When I realized that my attempts to make my English class interesting and enjoyable to my students were recognized by my principal, it led me to a whole new level of activity, creativity, and extra energy.

Speak to the heart. Find what is at the core of your audience's concerns. Keep your eyes and ears tuned to finding out those central, most important feelings, concerns, issues, or values, and speak to them directly. That is the key, the foundation, the secret to the art of motivational speaking.

HOW DID I GET INTO THIS IN THE FIRST PLACE?

BEING SELECTED TO GIVE A MOTIVATIONAL SPEECH

You're in your office, and you glance at the calendar. A date seems to pop off the page and call to you, somewhat menacingly. "Remember me?" the day seems to say, "I'm the day when you have to give that 'motivational' speech." You swallow reflexively. Your heartbeat seems to increase. "Oh, did I forget that?" you think, "It's coming. Soon. And I don't know what to do."

It isn't as if you chose to give that speech. It seems to have chosen you. Very few people go out of their way to seek opportunities to get up in front of large audiences and expound. Currently we are told that there are about 266,500,000 people in the United States. (I accessed the U.S. Bureau of the Census's site on the World Wide Web to check this.) How many of them would you guess are full-time public speakers? Not a very big percentage, would you agree? People who earn all or part of their living from public speaking are a tiny fraction of our population. That tiny fraction includes most of the few who actually seek the opportunity to speak in front of a group. Who are the rest of this small minority? It's easy to guess that people who want to sell something—an idea, a philosophy, a religious commitment, a product, some services—are the members of the group of sellers who actively seek audiences. If you are one of these people, you are likely to be highly motivated. In fact, your motivation may be strong enough to help you overcome any natural shyness you might have or any worry about your abilities or the smoothness of your technique. You're a committed believer in something, and the speech is simply your method of getting closer to your goal.

There are, however, others who will find themselves with a motivational speech on their calendars.

- ▪ *Your passion for the topic is well known.* Your reputation with regard to this topic is known to the meeting planner or his or her group or company. They want someone who will set them on fire about this topic, and you are clearly the person for the job.
- ▪ *Your values are seen as congruent with the group's values.* This is a group that doesn't want surprises. They want someone they know they'll agree with on the major issues. They hope that you can help them find energy about this particular topic.
- ▪ *You were drafted into the job.* Your boss at work told you that you've been elected to speak to the entire sales force next Thursday at 9:00 A.M., and he wants a real humdinger, too! Or your minister, priest, or rabbi asked you to address the couples club at the place you worship or to talk to the parents of the children at the Sunday School about the necessity for regular attendance. "How can I do this in a way that will really motivate?" you ask yourself.
- ▪ *You have had a unique experience or background that makes you the perfect person to motivate people who can identify with you.* For example, when you were in high school, you had to struggle to even qualify for the football team. You had a very difficult first year and broke two bones. Somehow, against all odds, in your second year, you found your way and eventually became the star of the team. You made the

key play in the most important game of the season. The coach at your old high school has called you and asked you to speak with this year's team about "sticking with the program and giving 110 percent effort." Or, you were a wounded veteran of the war in Vietnam. Despite losing a leg and spending years in rehabilitation, you became a jogger, a biker, and a world-class salesman. The president of your company has asked you to speak to this year's national sales meeting. People do find much motivation in stories by or about people who have conquered adversity. Although you know this, you don't want to make a big deal of your past experience and feel uncomfortable being asked to speak. You didn't have much choice, though, and the day is coming soon. "How can I survive this speech? How can I do it and still feel good about myself afterward?"

■ *You sought this opportunity yourself.* You are in sales. You sell anything from insurance to real estate, cars, or HMO programs. You've worked for quite a time trying to get the chance to speak to this group. If you really touch their hearts, you feel you'll get lots of new contacts and referrals. Or, you are filled with religious conviction. This group represents an opportunity to reach a group and begin their commitment or deepen their commitment in your faith. "How can I reach them in a way that will be authentic and not a turnoff?" you wonder, as you begin to prepare.

■ *You were asked to give this speech because you are a respected professional in this field.* You're seen, by the conference planners, as a model for those attending. Your unique contributions to the field give you much credibility. They want you to help those attending fight off the malaise of burnout and rediscover the "fire in their bellies" about your field. You're not sure you can do it. After all, you sometimes feel burned out, too. And, you think, "Who am I to tell them how to feel?"

■ *You are a professional speaker and trainer.* You've specialized in informative talks, humorous talks, or training sessions and seminars. This is one of your first forays into the field of motivational speaking. You're not sure how to go about making this leap. How will this be different from the trainings and speeches you've given so many times before?

▪ *You're a professional motivational speaker.* You've been doing this for years. You are reading this book because you'd like to get someone else's take on this business. How does this author see it? Does he have anything new to tell you? You've seen other speakers who lost their edge. They got complacent. They began giving the same talk, no matter what the group, year in and year out. Their speeches were once great. After a while they became merely good. Having repeated the same presentations so many times, the words come out devoid of passion and aliveness. As experienced professionals, they are masters of technique. They know what has worked for all these years and they trot out their techniques, their tried-and-true lines and bits and shtick. Oh, it works, all right, but the standing ovations are fewer, and something vital seems missing from their work. You're concerned that you don't end up this way. You are committed to staying fresh and alive to your work. So you read books on speaking, you attend other speaker's presentations, you belong to a professional organization like the National Speakers Association or Toastmasters International, and you go to meetings.

However you were selected, elected, or hired, you are facing the fact that you will soon be giving a motivational talk. It is important, however, to realize that the way you were chosen may have an impact on the success of your talk. If you were drafted, you must resolve to fight against the natural urge to let a bit of resentment or reluctance filter in to your presentation, in your word choice, or in the examples you use. Or it might slip in nonverbally in your posture or tone or eye contact (or lack of it!). If you were asked to do something that you truly do not want to do or believe in, or if you are asked to talk about something you find repugnant, that fact will become abundantly clear to your audience, unless you are the most consummately skilled actor in human history. People have an uncanny ability to sense this in a speaker.

MAKING SURE YOU'RE THE RIGHT PERSON FOR THE JOB

What should you do if you are chosen to do a talk that you think is inappropriate for you? It may be inappropriate because you don't agree with the topic, have difficulty feeling empathy with the group to whom you are to speak, or simply are convinced that you are not qualified to give this talk for whatever reason. The best thing you can do is to refuse such a job. Although this may sound obvious, I have often met people who told me they were forced, cajoled, or just plain ordered to give motivational talks that, because of these circumstances, turned out to be much less than motivational!

Help the person who selected you by suggesting more appropriate candidates if you can. But do not give that speech unless you find yourself in synch with the group, its goals and ideals, and with the topic and the position you are asked to represent. When you are approached to give a motivational talk, make sure that you do feel that you have some unique insight, special experience, appropriate perspective, or content that is of potential value to the intended audience. It is a disservice to an audience and to yourself to accept a speaking engagement that doesn't really fit you.

ACCEPTING THE STRETCH

The exception to this guideline would be when you are about to stretch yourself. You believe that you might not be qualified, in the strictest sense, but you are *qualifiable*. You are sure that you can prepare yourself more than adequately to fulfill the requirements of the engagement. This is an ethical dilemma: How do you gain the experience necessary to be a

confident and professional motivational speaker unless you
do stretch yourself by accepting a presentation you are not
yet totally prepared for? On the other hand, don't we owe it
to the meeting planner and to the intended audience to give
them the best possible speaker for their presentation? You
will have to cope with this dilemma if you are new to the
field of motivational speaking. One answer is to be forthcoming with the meeting planner: "Well, I've given many *informational* speeches in my career, Mr. Smith, and I've been
moving toward the motivational end of the business lately.
I'd love to do this presentation for you. I'm sure that I can do
a great job for you!" It's up to you how you decide to handle
this dilemma.

TURNING A "NO" INTO AN "I KNOW"

When turning an offered presentation down because it
doesn't fit you, it makes sense to help the meeting planner
find an alternate speaker. This is good because it's a win-win-
win! You win because (a) you'll feel very ethical and (b) the
meeting planner will be impressed with your forthrightness
and honesty and will be likely to consider you for a different
presentation and/or recommend you to others. This has happened to me a number of times over the years. In one case, a
company manager called me to do a workshop on stress management. Although my brochures clearly indicated that my
stress management presentations had to be a minimum of one
full day, he insisted that he "only had 45 minutes for this
kind of stuff." On further discussion, it became clear that he
did not value the topic himself and was simply caving in to
employee demands. He wanted to check this off his list with a
quick down-and-dirty workshop of little value. I explained to
him that, of all my topics, stress management was the most
volatile—because I believe that some people coming to the

workshop would be honestly seeking immediate help and such a short workshop would be more of a tease and less of a help than I felt was professionally appropriate. He kept insisting and even offered to raise my fee way beyond what I was asking. I still refused, quietly and politely. He was initially angry and frustrated and, after I gave him the names of several colleagues who spoke on the subject, decided to go with one of these other speakers. However, four weeks later, he called back with a request for me to do several weeks of training with his company! "I think I can really trust you to do a really good job for me on this," he said.

Refusing an inappropriate assignment is a win-win-win because the meeting planner and his or her audience wins by not having a presentation that doesn't fit their needs. And, finally, if you refer the meeting planner to several other potential speakers, you will be marketing for them as well as for your own future jobs. How does this work? Gratitude! The meeting planner is a busy person and is often struggling with a small list of potential speakers. If you were the one who was recommended to your meeting planner, he or she may not have any other people in mind. When you say, "I am not available for that date," or "I don't think there's a match between me and that topic," the meeting planner may be in a panic. When you add, "But let me recommend to you several speakers whom I personally know to be excellent," the panic subsides. Deep gratitude replaces it. I have gotten many jobs over the years from grateful meeting planners whom I first had to turn down because of schedule conflicts or because they originally called me for topics that just weren't ones that I could do appropriately. In addition, the speakers whom you recommend will almost always throw jobs your way in return for having recommended them. It makes sense, therefore, to keep a current list of all the speakers you've met whose work impressed you, along with their contact information.

WHAT DO I HAVE TO DO TO GET STARTED?

Your Meeting Planner's Goals

It sounds obvious that the speaker ought to make a very strong effort to discover the meeting planner's goals for the presentation. You've had a brief conversation, much of which was taken up with details about your fee, the date of the presentation, and how the planner heard of you. It is easy to assume that you really know what your meeting planner hopes to achieve with your speech. People may be speaking in platitudes or vague generalities. Certain key words may have different meanings for you than they have for your host. "I really want a shot in the arm for this group." "I'm looking for a really rousing, motivating talk. Get them up and going!" What does this mean to you? And are you sure your planner meant the same things? Most professional speakers invest the time up front in finding out as much about the client and his or her goals as possible.

Here are some possible areas of inquiry:

1. *What are the purposes of this meeting?* You will often have to be persistent, asking this question several times and/or in several different ways in order to get at the real goals of the meeting. There are often "show goals" given because the meeting planner wants to seem more professional or for other reasons that are not obvious. ("What would you like each participant to get at this meeting?" "If you could wave a magic wand at this meeting and get exactly what you want out of the meeting, what would that be like?")

2. *Can you describe the various groups that will be attending?* Here, you want to obtain information about the constituencies that will be in the room. For example, a schoolwide meeting might include only teachers and administrators, or it might also include guidance personnel, secretaries, groundskeepers, bus drivers, and so on. Is it a meeting of sales personnel or department managers?

Pitching your speech to the audience is not possible unless you have a clear handle on who they are.

3. *Are there any conflicts going on within this group or among some of the various groups that may attend?* Remember that your meeting planner may or may not be fully in touch with what is going on in the group.

4. *What was your past experience with a speaker or at the last meeting or conference?* This tells you if they are coming in with an "edge" such as, "I hope this speaker is more informed than the last one," or "I hope this speaker will keep us awake and laughing the way the last one did."

5. *What would you like to see them get at this meeting?* Check out whether the person calling you is representative of the group. Sometimes your contact person is really out of the loop, not in real contact with the feelings, issues, and concerns that are currently running through the group. That leads to the next question. Note that this is another reiteration of question one. It really is difficult to get a clear picture of what the goals are.

6. *Are you part of a committee that's planning this meeting? What was their process like?* You're trying to find out if there's unanimity in the group or if the conference theme—and possibly the choice of you as a speaker—was the product of conflict or power plays by a vocal but influential minority. Such events have occurred in my career, and you can find yourself giving a speech that, no matter the quality, cannot satisfy any but a small minority in the group. There's a famous poster that says,

"God So Loved the World, He Did Not Send a Committee!"

This quotation always provokes a response because people are aware of the frustrations and hidden agendas often associated with committees. Be extra alert when a committee is inviting you or planning the meeting.

7. *What will immediately precede my presentation?* You want to understand the mood, general energy level, and the kinds of thoughts and feelings the group may have as you begin

your talk. If they will have been sitting through a three-hour detailed explication of federal and state regulations, they will be impatient, tired, distractible, and generally unreceptive. You might wish to suggest a different timing for your talk, refuse the job, or, more likely, plan a method of structuring your presentation that can liven things up.

8. *What will immediately follow my presentation?* You're exploring what the mood, expectation, or energy level of the group may be—for example, will they be impatiently waiting for lunch or dinner? Will you be the last speaker of a three-day conference when the audience is desperate to get home? Are you the opening speaker at a long-awaited sales meeting when everyone has heard that the company has exceeded its sales targets? Will the school board be announcing, after your presentation, that 50 teachers will be let go this year?*

9. *If you chose me because of my reputation or some of my writings or because some members of the group saw me speaking previously, what, specifically, did you like most about what you saw, heard, or read?* That is your attempt to satisfy their unspoken expectations.

10. *What can you tell me about previous speakers? Who did you have before me? What did you like most* and *least about them?* This will give you a very solid clue about what they are really seeking in a motivational speaker.

Other Ways of Getting Information from Your Client

These ten areas of needed information can sound like an interrogation. Don't make the first phone call too long or too onerous. It is better to get this information in a second or even a third phone call, after you've completed your negotia-

---

*Incredible as it may seem, this actually happened to me, giving a school opening address in a medium-sized city in the Midwest! The group of 900 teachers all knew that the list was forthcoming after my talk. You can imagine their attitude toward hearing a rousing motivational talk at that moment!

tions (if any) about honorarium, travel expenses, and any other details that you may have. We use a written questionnaire (see Figure 2.1) to gather much of the information.

In addition to the questionnaire, ask your contact person to send you all the written material possible about the group, its history, and its goals. If it's a company, association, or school or institution, ask them to send you the kind of material usually sent to a new hire or prospective employee or investor. Ask for their house newsletter or magazine and for any articles about them that have appeared in any publications in the past two years.

Go on to the Internet and use several search engines to find information about this group. With a bit of persistence, you can find out eye-opening material that can be of great benefit as you plan your talk. For example, I recently had a secondary school system in the Midwest as a client. They wanted a talk about the "workplace skills necessary in the 21st century." In two hours on the Internet I found the following: The school superintendent was job-hunting; the dates of construction of their several high schools; the high schools' team names and mascots, complete with logos; a famous astronaut was one of their graduates; pictures of their school administrators and several teachers; the names of about three of their programs that had been selected for honors regionally and nationally; their test scores were rather depressed; and finally, information about two court cases pending against them by local citizens. None of this information was offered to me by the meeting planner! Was it helpful? Of course! I grabbed the pictures and logos off the Internet and placed each one on one of my presentation slides. I put the astronaut's picture on one slide along with the question, "What did his teachers think he needed to know when he graduated from this school in the 1950s?" That was perfect for the lead into my topic, where I would be talking about how difficult it is to predict the future jobs skills we'll need. Knowing about the test scores helped me not to put my foot in my mouth in this sensitive area. I did not have to talk about scores, though I might have, had I not seen this.

Again going out on the World Wide Web, I researched the topic I had been asked to speak on and found more material than I could possibly use. I found research for and against the study that they were using. I found clear analyses, pro and con, for some of the programs they were already running in their schools. By reading the supporters and attackers, I was able to make the facts in my speech much tighter and more accurate and phrase them in ways less liable to misunderstanding or attack. By reading such material, I could get a sympathetic understanding of the positions taken by educators on this vital topic and become more prepared to offer new insights and positions that could bridge the controversies my audience was already contending with. A public speaker, says Joel Weldon, is an "information utility." As such, he or she has the responsibility to give fresh information, cutting-edge ideas, and useful and accurate data. Conducting this kind of preparation ensures you can live up to that charge.

Remember, once you get up in front of the group, it's too late to get any more information—your talk is supposed to be on target. So, it makes a considerable amount of sense—and you'll find it very reassuring as you prepare to deliver the talk—if you have as much information as possible about the group, its mood, its recent history, its level of motivation, its goals, and the best possible information about your topic as well. Figure 2.1 is a prepresentation questionnaire, which should be sent to the company or professional association once you have been contracted by them. Figure 2.2 (on page 29) is a listing of materials that will help you to customize your presentation for the group. This should be sent to your client with the prepresentation questionnaire.

Figure 2.1

PREPRESENTATION QUESTIONNAIRE

Company or Professional Association: _____

Date of Presentation: _____

*This questionnaire is provided to help us **customize** the presentation to meet your goals for the day. Please take a few minutes to answer only the applicable questions, and return the form as soon as possible. You can use the back of this sheet to expand any answer if necessary.*

1. What are your *specific objectives* for this presentation?

    a. _____

    _____

    _____

    _____

    b. _____

    _____

    _____

    _____

    c. _____

    _____

    _____

    _____

2. What areas do you hope to improve the most?

    _____

    _____

    _____

3. What are *you* most proud of about your organization (company, group, unit)?

    _____

    _____

    _____

4. Name and title of my introducer: _____. Please have my introducer talk with me just prior to the presentation to work out any last-minute details.

5. What is planned immediately *prior* to my presentation (speakers, invocations, prayers, announcements, a break, etc.)? If I am doing several presentations, let me know what precedes each one. Please use a separate piece of paper.

_____

_____

6. What is planned immediately *after* my presentation?

_____

_____

7. Starting time for my presentation: _____ A.M. _____ P.M.

   Ending time for my presentation: _____ A.M. _____ P.M.

8. Who are the other speakers (if any) on the program?

   Speaker: _____ Topic: _____

   Speaker: _____ Topic: _____

   Speaker: _____ Topic: _____

(If there is a speaker who will be covering the same topic area[s] as I, it would be helpful if you'd provide that speaker's office phone number so I can coordinate my presentation and not have too much overlap in what we will offer the group.)

9. Is there any recent history in the group that I should be aware of (negotiations, strikes or threatened job actions, recent death of a coworker, local controversy, legal battles, sudden stock price changes, attempted corporate takeovers, etc.)?*

_____

_____

_____

---

*The actual wording of these items will change according to the type of client you are serving. For example, if you are dealing with a corporation, this form will probably fit well. If it is a governmental agency, a school, a professional association, etc., each item will require a bit of rethinking and tinkering. For a school group, the "stock prices" and other items might be replaced by "death of a student, change in local funding, etc."

10. Are there any taboo topics to be avoided?

_____

_____

_____

11. Do you have any suggestions to help me make this the best presentation ever?

_____

_____

_____

12. What was the last similar or comparable presentation (in topic, goals, format, or timing) to this group?

_____

_____

_____

   a. What was the group's reaction or response to that presentation?

_____

_____

_____

   b. What did _you_ like _best_ about it?

_____

_____

_____

   c. What did _you_ like _least_ about it?

_____

_____

_____

   d. What wasn't offered or done that you felt was needed?

_____

_____

_____

13. Who will meet me at the airport? _____

    Daytime phone number of that person __(   )_____

    Home phone number of that person __(   )_____

14. What is the exact location of the meeting? (Send step-by-step directions, map, building diagram, etc.)

15. If I have any emergencies or problems on my way to the program, whom should I contact (include home and business phone numbers)?

    _____

    _____

    _____

If I am delayed enroute, I will make every possible attempt to get to you. Check alternate flights. I will also call your office or home phones and probably attempt to leave a message for you at the airport message center or airline counter. (It would help to have the local airport's message or paging phone number _(   )_____ or __(   )_____)*

16. Approximate number of attendees: _____. Describe these attendees in terms of their job descriptions and/or other demographic information which would help me to understand and/or relate to them. (Example: 500 total: 25 percent executive level, 25 percent clerical, 40 percent line managers and 10 percent selected production line workers.)

    _____

    _____

    _____

    _____

    _____

17. Names of any employee organization leaders who will be present:

    a. _____

           Name   Title

    b. _____

           Name   Title

    c. _____

           Name   Title

---

*This item has really reassured many clients. The meeting planner does not want to stand up in front of 400 people to announce that the session is canceled.

Figure 2.2

MATERIALS THAT WILL HELP ME TO CUSTOMIZE MY PRESENTATION FOR YOUR GROUP

1. Is there anything very exciting (such as a corporate team that is winning, a major new product you've announced, a great new client, a major sale you've achieved, etc.) which, if I mention it, would bring delight to your audience?

2. Send me the names and logos of your products or services. I will be using these to create new transparencies built into my presentation. The sooner I can get these, the better.

3. Are there any employees, managers, or others associated with your company or association who have had articles in the newspaper about their accomplishments? Please send me their names and copies of the articles. (For example, are some employees engaged in a project helping local youth programs?)

4. Please send any announcements, brochures, flyers, etc., that you send to the participants describing the meeting and my session.*

5. Please send me photographs of four to six individuals who will be attending the meeting and whom you consider to be "unsung heroes." With each photo, it would help to have a short paragraph telling me of their accomplishments. I will be using these photos in my presentation; please do *not* tell these people about this, so the surprise will be complete. Try to make sure you're picking people from each area of the group, company or school, and from each type or category of job.

6. Please send me a copy of any similar program you may have held in the past.

7. Please send me any orientation material describing your company or association or school that you would provide to new hires.

8. Please send me copies of any articles in the media about your organization or company. Include copies of your in-house journal or newspapers for the past year, if possible.

---

*No matter how hard you work at good communication, sometimes there will be a meeting planner who will hear what he or she wants to hear, and you may discover that your presentation is being described in very different terms (or even with a different topic!) from those you think you've discussed and agreed to.

PREPARING FOR THE PRESENTATION

You've received your questionnaire back, and you've also been in contact with the client exploring his or her goals for the meeting. No matter how well your meeting planner understands the group he or she represents, you've only got one person's opinion, point of view, and set of values with which to work. Most times that has proven to be quite adequate, but there are times when you'll discover that there were minority opinions out there that would have been good to know while preparing your talk.

Most professional speakers can tell you horror stories about times when they were blind-sided by incorrect or incomplete information or their meeting planner's bias or lack of knowledge. There you are, in front of the group with egg on your face—not a good place to be. To avoid this and to make a thoroughly professional presentation, you may want to call in the big guns: the most powerful information-gathering techniques for the motivational speaker.

The Most Powerful Information-Gathering Techniques for the Motivational Speaker

A questionnaire filled out by your meeting planner or the committee is a good but limited tool for gathering information. This technique is limited because many people do not invest much time in filling them out. In addition, you've had to make the questionnaire generic before really getting to know this client and its specific characteristics. Some people use a questionnaire sent to numbers of employees, but I have found this almost useless because (1) you get few replies and (2) people will give "normative" replies—what they think you want to hear or what they think the boss wants them to say. And this is true even for so-called "anonymous" questionnaires!

There are other techniques that can produce information that will really help you to fine-tune your presentation to the actual needs and situation of your client. These techniques are the key informant phone interview and the key informant on-site interview.

The Key Informant Phone Interview

Ask your meeting planner to send you a list of 10 to 15 employees in a cross-section of job categories of the group that will be attending your presentation. Ask for their office phone numbers, e-mail addresses, and other contact information including their job titles and what divisions or units they represent. You want to find out about each one—how representative of their group, office, job category, division, or the like are they likely to be? Some meeting planners or clients will consciously or unconsciously select only people whom they like, agree with, work with well, and so on. This will necessarily limit the information you receive. Set up an interview schedule of times you will be available, and ask employees to call you or, alternatively, find out their schedule of availability and set up appointments to call them. These appointments will help minimize "playing phone tag," which will be quite frustrating and counter-productive.

Create a list of questions you'll ask each interviewee. Conduct two or three interviews, and, based on the responses you've received, revise these questions. (I have found that I almost totally revise the list after the second or third interview because I now have enough information to ask more intelligent and focused questions.) Make sure that some of your questions focus on the needs and wants that are being satisfied and those that are not being satisfied in the person's experience.

At the beginning of the interview, make sure the person understands who you are, what you are doing, and why—and especially that you will keep his or her answers totally confidential. I always tell my interviewees that, unless they want me to specifically quote them, I will remove any identifying information from their answers before I use what I learn to develop my presentation. Keeping your word on this is absolutely necessary to maintain your own credibility!

The Key Informant On-Site Interview

This is an extension and deepening of the telephone interview. Sometimes I have conducted the phone interview, and then, because I did not get what I needed—perhaps the company is just too large or complex—I've followed up with an on-site visit.

You can reasonably interview between six and eight people in one day—if your schedule has been set up well by your local contact. Try to do these interviews on the person's home turf—in their office or workplace, where they are likely to feel most comfortable. Exceptions must be made when the individual would rather meet you on neutral ground, a quieter location, or the like.

Again, you must offer the person your guarantee of confidentiality. Make sure he or she is voluntarily being interviewed. The person who is ordered to report to you will not provide useful information.

Don't let these interviews go more than 30 minutes. I have found that 15 to 20 minutes is more than sufficient to get a good idea about how they feel about their jobs, discover what they think the issues are in the company or in their work unit, and find out what they think needs to be done to improve things at work.

Don't forget to thank your interviewees. I always remember to send them a thank-you note and even copies of my latest book or some other item of value to let them know that their help was truly appreciated. Word of this gets around the organization and makes people much more delighted to come to your presentation and listen to you.

Sample Questions for Key Informant Interviews (Corporate):
1. Setting the tone for the interview.
   a. How long have you worked with the company? (Or how long have you been in this job?)
   b. Help me understand the kinds of things you do in your job. What does your job encompass?
   c. How have things been going lately?
   d. Is there anything you'd like to ask me?
2. Getting into the meat of the interview.
   a. How do you feel about your job?
   b. What are you most proud of in the way you do your job?
   c. What are the two or three best things about your job?
   d. What are the two or three least enjoyable or least satisfying things about your job?
   e. Where are the hangups or problems that most frustrate you?
   f. What are the parts of your job that bring you the most pleasure?
   g. What are the biggest or most important problems you think the company is facing at this time?
   h. What are the biggest opportunities you think are available to the company right now?
   i. What is one question you wish someone would ask out loud at the next meeting of your department?
3. Finishing the interview.
   a. If you had a magic wand and could simply wave it and make changes in (the company, your job, your office, your coworkers, your supervisor, or the like), what would you wave it to get?
   b. (Similar question.) If you suddenly became the final authority and could make any decision to make things better here, what decisions would you make, or which new policies or procedures would you put in place?

    c. If you could design my speech for me, what would you be sure to put in it?

    d. Can you tell me about something a colleague or coworker has done that you think is particularly impressive or worthy of positive notice?

    e. What are your supervisor's three best characteristics?

Making Sense of the Information You've Gathered

You will find, in most key informant interviews, that the information you receive will be quite consistent. Most of your informants will confirm each other's data with some notable exceptions. When the information is consistent, you can have confidence that any conclusions you draw from it can be trusted. You'll find out what the real agendas are, whether or not people are generally satisfied with their jobs and with the conditions under which they work. You'll get great real-life examples that can be used—with your respondent's permission, of course—as positive stories in your motivational talk.

    When you get inconsistent information (example: fourteen people say that Mr. Jones is extremely nice to work with and one person tells you nothing but horror stories about him), you have to examine the biases of the few dissenting respondents. How representative are they? Do they have an ax to grind? (Be wary of dismissing their opinions—they may be the "lone voice in the wilderness" that brings the real truth!)

    It is amazing how powerful some of these questions have been in producing answers that illuminated what was really going on in a company or an organization. There is often such an impenetrable wall between upper management and others below them in the company that these different constituencies have totally opposite views of what is really going on. People may, rightly or wrongly, think that if they really told the truth as they see it, they would be fired, demoted, or otherwise harmed. They may have become skilled in avoiding the truth, skirting it, denying it, or otherwise distancing themselves from anyone who does speak it.

The Key Informant Tells It Like It Is

Hans Christian Andersen's fairy tale, *The Emperor's New Clothes,* is a fascinating example of what everyone knows will *not* happen when the truth is told. Some con men have sold the Emperor on some imaginary fabric that is supposedly so very beautiful that anyone wearing it is instantly the best-dressed person possible; however, it will be invisible to anyone who is incompetent and undeserving of his or position. The Emperor buys this idea, caught up in their web of deceit (and afraid to admit that he himself can't see the fabric!). He purchases the fabric and has them make him grand garments to wear at a ball. Of course, he appears in front of the court totally naked. Because he is the Emperor, and because the courtiers fear for their positions, no one has the courage to tell him that he is naked. He parades about, and all the courtiers remark loudly on the beauty of his new vestments. Only a little boy, innocent and fearless, dares tell the truth. "Your Majesty," he cries, "You are naked!" And in Andersen's sweet but improbable story, the boy is rewarded by the Emperor for his candor and courage.

All of us, and certainly all the employees in the modern corporation, with down-sizing menacing ever present in the background, know that the boy would be killed or imprisoned by a real Emperor. So, too, they know that the boss must not be told the truth if it is unpleasant. "The program that you, the boss, so staunchly advocated last year has lost us our lead in the marketplace. Our competitors are laughing at us, and our customers are fleeing in droves." Who wants to be the bearer of such news?

By conducting a good key-informant interview, you can discover some of the truth of an organization and become empowered to make a motivational talk that will really speak to the main issues confronting the corporation. As the outside consultant or speaker, it may be your task to be the one with the courage to say the truth. Make sure, though, that your client wants this kind of service. I don't believe that it is my job to do things *to* my clients; rather, I want to do things *for* them. If you ever want to be invited back or recommended elsewhere, you must not take the arrogant position of, "This stuff is good for you, even if you don't want any."

Getting clear and accurate information in advance can help you avoid putting your foot in your mouth. When you don't know what's really going on, it is easy to find yourself getting laughs you didn't expect or desire as you innocently parrot the party line that was given to you by the boss, the meeting planner, and the brochures you were sent. If you are in that situation, it becomes clear to your audience that you know less than they do rather than having the new or special insights they crave. You'll lose your audience in a hurry if you are not "in the know."

Ethics of Interviewing

It is most important to note that you have several big responsibilities if you do conduct these interviews:

1. *Keeping the specific sources of your information confidential.* Which interviewee said what must never be revealed even inadvertently. "A number of people I interviewed indicated that they felt . . ." is how you might phrase some of your conclusions in your talk.
2. *Keeping the totality of the information you develop confidential.* You do not want to give away trade secrets or give any advantage to a competitor or in any other way cause harm to your client.
3. *Making sure to focus on the positive.* Especially with regard to negative information you receive, your talk must focus

on the positive, on what can be done instead of what problems there are. If your interviews lead you to focus your talk on problems only, you will hardly motivate your group—instead you will depress and frighten them. That is not your job. It is your business, as a motivational speaker, to uplift, enlighten, make possible, instill hope.

4. *When interviewing employees, remembering that you are not an agent of the employer.* Nor are you an agent of the employees. Do not take sides, carry tales, make hints, or give advice about policies or programs. Because you are the motivational speaker, your words carry much more weight than they do when you are just a private individual. Some chance remark of yours can end up traveling around the group and can be used as a bludgeon to harm others or make someone's point. "The consultant said I was right!" Your time for input into the group is during your speech. At that time, your comments are public, and everyone can hear them, evaluate them, decide to follow them, or defend against them.

3 WHAT MOTIVATES PEOPLE?

If you plan on giving motivational speeches, you would do well to become more aware of what motivates the people to whom you will be speaking. People have many motivations, some stronger than others. In fact, there is a *hierarchy* of motivations. For example, one might want to improve one's ability to speak French and yet, no matter how much you want that, if you are starving, your motivation to eat will be much stronger and more immediately acted upon than your desire for foreign language lessons. Your desire to save your own life is strong but may be superseded by your desire to save your child.

Motivations come in varieties: There are positive and negative motivations; social, physical, emotional, spiritual, and intellectual motivations. There are greed, fear, lust, love, altruism, and the desire for safety. If your audience perceives that one or more of these areas is deficient or unfulfilled, or if they are even experiencing pain in this aspect of their lives, and you provide in your speech some road toward fulfillment of that need, you will have motivated them, and they will not soon forget you and your message. Your speech does not have to fulfill the need or solve the problem—it simply has to offer a view of how to solve the problem or a route toward the fulfillment of that need or convince those listening that they have the power to satisfy that need at some time in the future with a reasonable expenditure of time and energy.

Motivation is not something that you do TO people, it is something you do WITH people. It is not a paint job that you apply to the external surface of individuals or a group of people. Real motivation comes from inside the person, so the motivational speaker, to be truly effective, has to understand, search out, and tap into those already existing motivations. People do not enter the conference room or auditorium with their motivations neutral, blank, and unformed. The fact that they are entering the room—or have arrived at the building—is a result of motivations. It is the height of arrogance to imagine that you are going to take a group of people and, without their participation and consent, motivate them in a direction they do not already want to go. Even accomplished demagogues (Adolf Hitler, Huey Long, Father Coughlin, and Louis Farrakhan are great 20th century examples) who seem to mesmerize their audiences or famous charismatic figures (think of famous politicians, rock stars, or televangelists) are successful at least partially because they are skilled at understanding (and implying their ability to satisfying) the unmet needs clamoring to be fulfilled in the populations they reach.

Let us look at some typical examples, one from the public schools and one from a corporate environment.

A PUBLIC SCHOOLS EXAMPLE: WEST HILLS UNIFIED SCHOOL DISTRICT OPENING DAY CEREMONIES, AUGUST 28

A group of teachers are gathering in the high school auditorium for the traditional opening day of school meetings.

Mrs. Ellen Callaway, a young, first-year elementary teacher, is driving to the school. She is filled with eagerness, delight, and worry; she's *delighted* that she found a job so near her new apartment. When her husband moved to this area for his new job, she *worried* whether she'd find work at all. She heard that teaching jobs were scarce near this city and is quite *relieved* that she landed a good position with this school system in an upscale suburb. She's *anxious* about meeting new people, *worried* that she'll fit in, and quite *concerned* that she makes a good impression. "I *wonder* if I'll find any friends here?" she thinks as she hunts for a parking space in a rapidly filling parking lot behind the school. She misses the friends with whom she did her practice teaching. She enters the building, picks up her "hello badge," and makes a beeline for the coffee and donuts table. The line is long and slow. Several people start conversations with her. They invite her to sit with them. She relaxes a bit. She enters the auditorium early, with her new acquaintances, and takes a seat in the third row. They chatter excitedly about the new year. They tell her about the school superintendent whom they hate because of several very unpopular decisions she made last year. Ellen realizes that to keep her new friends she'll have to be careful of what she says about the administration.

Carl Fenster makes his way into the building. He teaches high school science. He's been there almost forever. He shakes hands with an old friend, waves at two colleagues, nods toward his department chairman with whom he went camping this summer as they have for 20 years. Picking up his hello badge, he puts it in his pocket, refusing to wear it. By doing so, he joins a silent fraternity of resisters who populate the aging faculty in the district. Those "in the know" would never even think of wearing one as it would seem like a surrender to the superintendent against whom they had a job action last winter. He stops to have a cup of coffee with two buddies. They talk about retirement. Mr. Fenster is two years from retirement and he can't wait. "I've got to tough it out," he thinks, "just two more years, two more years." He waits until the very last moment before going in to the auditorium. He stands in the back. If he can get away with it, he will not sit during the proceedings at all. An assistant principal, Joe Demp, who used to be Mr. Fenster's student 15 years ago, comes up and says, "Sorry, Carl, they've told me that everyone has to take a seat. Will you do that for me?" he asks apologetically. Carl gives him a look somewhere between pity and contempt and climbs over the ropes in the back and sits in an area that is clearly marked as closed to seating. They are trying to get the group to sit up front and close together, and Carl has no intention of honoring that wish. The assistant principal sighs helplessly. Four of Carl's friends climb over the ropes and sit with him in the very back. One of them pulls the ropes down so that even more people coming in will sit in the back.

Down front, the presenter seems busy with his table, adjusting the overhead projector and fiddling with some other equipment. The school board president and two board members are sitting down front on the far left and talking to the superintendent. The superintendent, Imogene Teuscher, is attempting to look interested but seems clearly distracted, her eyes darting from one corner of the room to another. She is worried. She knows her support base is fading rapidly on the board and feels that this is her "make it or break it" year. She's brought in this motivational speaker because he came highly recommended, and she's banking on him making a great start to the year. Behind her are sitting two of her associate superintendents, both of whom are hoping to get her job when the ax falls, which they judge is likely to happen this year. Neither gets up to help organize the very slow seating process until Ms. Teuscher turns around and suggests that they go to the back and encourage the latecomers to get seated. She does this with a bit more acid in her tone than she intends. The school board president winces, and the superintendent catches that from the corner of her eye. She gets up and shuffles her papers, approaching the podium.

Two math teachers, eighth and ninth grades respectively, take their seats in the far right aisle. They take out lesson plan books and class lists and begin writing. They murmur to each other in voices dripping with sarcasm, "A *motivational* speaker! Let's get ready to get motivated!" "Yeah." Actually, they like motivational speakers. The woman who spoke to them last year was funny and touching, and they really enjoyed the experience. Yet, they know that it is uncool in the current school climate to be positive about these things.

Steve Grolier, teacher's union president and junior high English teacher, sits near the last "official" row with several other union officers. He is annoyed by the fact that his union was not consulted about the choice of keynote speaker or any other part of the program. He actually believes in motivational speakers and thinks they can really make a difference for his members' feelings of job satisfaction but is opposed to the top-down methods of choosing them. This speaker has become, for him, a symbol of his disempowerment.

A group of seven teachers who arrived early are seated together in the tenth row right. They've all got coffee and Danish and are talking quietly among themselves. They've taught together for a long time. They love their jobs; they love the kids; and they've been looking forward to the start of the year. They don't even care who is superintendent. "The fact is, we can outlast any superintendent. We have tenure. They don't!" This group lives almost in their own private world at one end of their school and feel insulated from such problems. They engage in the talk about the superintendent and such, but you can tell by their lack of energy about it that this is not a major concern of theirs.

Darrin Tyler sits alone. He came in alone, spoke to no one, took no coffee. He walked desultorily down the aisle and found a seat away from everyone. As the auditorium filled, no one chose to sit near him for no one knows him well. He is a loner. Sullenly, he stares at the stage with an unfocused, resigned expression. He teaches vocational education and driver training. He feels walled off from everyone, including the other two vocational education teachers in the building. He is infuriated by the thought of a memo he received from an assistant superintendent quoting a study of drivers' education that seemed to indicate that such programs were completely ineffective in changing teen driving behavior. The memo implied that the program was being considered for termination. He is even more upset that the other drivers' education teachers have not included him in their discussion of that memo.

Tim Guaraldo stands by the side of the auditorium with two other custodians. The supervisor told him that everyone has to attend this meeting. "I'm not a teacher!" he protested, "Why the heck do I have to be in there?" "Just shut up and go," he was told. He plans to sneak out the back as soon as things start.

The rear two rows are the private reserve of the high school and junior high school physical education department. All the P.E. teachers and coaches gather there. They hold their coffee and talk in loud voices about games past, present, and planned. Several have newspapers that they will open to the sports section during the keynote address. That's their way of saying, "Hey, this stuff is not for me. I'm immune."

Martina Vasquez sits with three other school secretaries in the fourth row. She is thrilled to be there. This is the first year that classified personnel have been invited to attend with the professional staff. "I can't wait," she says to her friends, "I heard these things are really good. This guy," pointing to the keynote speaker, "I read his résumé when it came in the office. He's written three books!"

There's your audience. Go up and down the aisles, and you'll find more like them with such complicated sets of feelings. You look out at the audience, a sea of faces, sitting in clumps well separated one from the other. The ropes at the back have not worked in bringing the group together. Your heart is pounding. A bell in the hallway begins insistent ringing. The superintendent stands at the podium and taps the microphone. The group still talks noisily. She asks for their attention, tapping on a water glass on the podium. Finally, the group quiets. There will be the flag salute, the invocation, a brief welcome from the school board president. The superintendent will make a few (you hope) remarks. And then you're on. And you've got to *motivate* them!

A CORPORATE EXAMPLE: PRICE-O-MATIC, INC., FALL SALES MEETING, MARRIOTT HOTEL, AUGUST 28

Four hundred salespeople, team leaders, and managers are due to arrive this morning at the Marriott for the fall sales meeting.

Prentice Darman, sales manager for the Northwest, arrives early to help set up the room and make sure that the hotel's banquet staff has everything done as planned. He enters and finds almost nothing done by the night crew. Almost frantic, Prentice runs around the hotel, seeking staff members to help him get things going. This is his meeting, his chance to shine, to impress the National Sales Director, Dana Tisbury. He finds the banquet manager who tries to soothe him. "We'll get everything in shape right away, I promise you." He still seems frantic with worry.

Workers enter the meeting room and begin setting up. A technician begins doing mike checks, "Test, test, test. Test, test, test." Four people are sitting, alone, well dispersed around the room. Each munches absent-mindedly on a donut and sips coffee. Prentice hurries out to the lobby to see about setting up the registration tables. His secretary, Norma, has arrived struggling in with a large heavy carton of materials. "Nothing was done!" he says exasperatedly, "They're just starting to set up." "It's OK, we'll get it done," Norma answers, unflappably. He counts on her ability to cope with these crises. Her calm response works, calming him somewhat. "I'll see what I can do." She bustles off. He begins taking items out of the box and setting them on the tables.

The coffee and donuts setup appears and is stocked by two hotel workers, chatting in Spanish. Just then, Dave Blount, his counterpart from the Chicago office, arrives. They've been friendly rivals for years. "Hey, Prentice, how's it going?" "We're getting it under control," Prentice replies, affecting more calm than he feels.

Tim Dane and his wife Darla arrive. They are a sales team from Miami. First to arrive, as usual, they've got the reputation as eager beavers and are liked as well as envied. "Can we help?" asks Darla, already starting to straighten up the tables and laying out name tags and conference packets. Darla and Tim have enviable sales stats, have been featured in the company's in-house sales force magazine, *PriceRight*. Prentice thinks, "Gotta watch those two, they're headed up there. Maybe I could get them transferred to my territory?"

"Looking forward to this meeting," says Tim. "I know we're going to have a great fall. I've been doing test calls of selected clients, and it looks great!"

Sitting in his car in the parking lot, Gary Gumpert lights another cigarette. He's never late for a meeting. He makes sure of that by coming extra early. He doesn't want to seem too gung-ho, so he sits and waits for just the right moment to enter. He watches cars enter the lot. When he sees enough of the people he knows, he'll go in. "What a drag of a day," he thinks, "more rah-rah crap. Look, you can either sell or you can't. We don't need motivation, we need more support from the main office, faster processing of our orders, and a production line that responds to special orders more effectively." He hunches down in his seat and takes a drag on his cigarette. "No one will say that, will they? Just suck up to the bosses, and we'll all applaud. What a bore!"

Throughout the meeting, he will fidget, look at his watch, sigh ostentatiously, read a magazine only half hidden in his conference program, pass little sly notes to his buddies sitting nearby, and make an apparently endless series of snide comments about the program. He's got his own coterie, his buddies, the audience he plays to, and they all enjoy his antics as a counterpoint to the main program and as a signal that they are their own people, immune to control from above.

The speaker is up on the platform, making last-minute adjustments to some transparencies laid out on the table next to the overhead projector. His back is toward the audience. On the platform with him, seated facing the audience, are the National Sales Director,

Dana Tilsbury, and her direct supervisor, Carlo Gutier-
rez, Vice President for North American Sales, and the
CEO, Richard Trent. They are speaking animatedly,
occasionally gesturing toward the audience. Dana peri-
odically glances at Prentice and at the speaker and raises
her eyebrows as if to say, "Is this guy ready? Are we
going to have a success today or what?" This seems to
goad Prentice into more frantic activity—shuttling
between little visits to the speaker to ask if he needs
anything and rushing to the back of the room to try to
seat the many salespeople standing there with coffee
networking. "Bring your coffee to your seats, folks," he
says, with a pasted-on smile, "the program is about to
begin." Few, if any, heed him.

Four men and one woman, the Omaha contingent,
arrive together, pick up some coffee, and carefully
select seats in the very front of the room. They take
laptops out of their carrying cases and begin compar-
ing schedules on their contact management programs.
The company's most successful sales team, they know
that they will be recognized today, for the third year in
a row, with cash awards, Hawaii vacations, and
engraved plaques. They are very alert, very present. As
they entered the room they made a handshaking tour
of the room, connecting with managers, assistant managers, and the second- and third-place sales teams
whom they beat to win the top honors this year. During the meeting, two of them will type notes on their
laptops quietly, quickly, and with almost ferocious
concentration.

Sheldon Grabow, a salesman from Columbus, sits
alone, apart from his team. He was demoted two years ago
for consistently coming in lower than his sales targets.
Because he was their former star, his supervisor has cut
him some slack, aware that in the last three years, Sheldon
has been through a divorce, gall bladder surgery, and an
IRS audit. Sheldon seems morose, distracted. He does not
look around the room. His shoulders slump, his brow fur-
rowed, as he desultorily reads the program.

Jaime Delgado, recently passed over for a promotion he had his sights on, saunters into the room, a half smile on his face. He waves at a few colleagues and stops to speak with Nancy Mitstein, a supervisor who was in the same incoming "class" at the company training center when they were both hired four years ago. "Got your résumé out, Jaime?" she asks, knowing the answer has to be in the positive. "Of course, Nance, and things are lookin' good." He is lying. There hasn't been even a nibble. He's worried because he took such a hard position with his boss about losing the promotion. Everyone expects him to leave soon, and his continued presence is beginning to be remarked on. He sits with a regional sales director from Texas, schmoozing him with studied casualness, and remains seated near him as the meeting begins, although his group, the New England team, is seated across the room.

Alice Marquardt, office manager at the Des Moines factory, steps up to the podium and approaches the speaker. "I read about you in the program. I'm especially interested in what you have to say about the lack of motivational effect of employee pay raises." You look up from your transparencies and grin at her, shaking her hand. Reading her name tag, you say, "Alice, thank you for your interest. I will be directly touching on that in my talk. Perhaps, if you want to discuss this further, we can sit together at the luncheon after the session?"

The lights dim slightly, and, at the podium, Prentice taps a water glass with a pen, *plink, plink, plink!*, coughs into the microphone and begins, "Good morning! Welcome to Sales Sensation Twenty-Three! The 23rd annual fall sales convention of Price-O-Matic!" The group obliges with applause. In the back of the room, three men, standing with cups of coffee, check their watches and glance furtively at the exit.

"And now let me welcome to the podium, our leader, our visionary, the nationally celebrated CEO of Price-O-Matic, Richard Trent." The applause swells. The meeting has begun. The keynote speaker (that's you!)

sits on the platform smiling, small beads of perspiration beginning to show on your forehead.

Mr. Trent is supposed to speak for about five minutes, welcoming the group. He is scheduled for a substantive talk in the afternoon session. Instead, he forgets his time limit, being the CEO, and launches into a 25-minute verbal essay on the toughness of the competition in the price marker business, the difficulty of staying on top of the technological changes in the industry, and the problem of keeping a solid profit margin in the face of rising salaries and wages. He hints that downsizing may be an alternative. He falls into "bird-walking"— a kind of rambling reminiscence that seems to have no point. Suddenly he seems to remember that there's a meeting and an agenda. He introduces your introducer. Now the keynote speaker is about to be introduced— that's you!—and you've got to *motivate* them!

GROUPS ARE NEVER HOMOGENEOUS

Any group—teachers, salespeople, police, middle managers, church members—is really just a collection of individuals each carrying his or her own motivations, feelings, personal history, values, concerns, fears, prejudices, hopes, desires, and goals. From the examples above, you might have noted that people, given a chance to self-select freely, will tend to organize themselves informally and/or formally into groups sharing similar motivations and values. Depending on their personalities, they will feel more able or less able to differ from their group on the particulars of those values and goals. Yet, given a certain group history, they will tend to share particular attitudes and feelings, hopes and responses. In the school example, the superintendent seems to be the focus of much feeling that is simmering just below the surface of the group. It's one of those situations in which *everyone publicly pretends not to know what they privately know.* In the corporate example, motivation of individuals seems to be related directly to their success within the company or their anticipation of future success. Groups coalesce because they may have to work together (a "team"—which may or may not consist of people who want to work together and have mutual respect and common goals), because they live near each other (the "car pool"), have a common enemy, share politics or life condition (single parents, members of a minority group), share a job title, and so on. Within groups, subgroups form and re-form as time goes on. And, always, there are loners, newbies, rejects, dissidents, people going through some dramatic life change, or others who do not fit in. All of them are motivated, but not all are motivated in just the way that the meeting planner(s) desire.

Some are motivated to be there, participate enthusiastically, be a part of the group, company, school, association, and do their utmost to carry out its goals effectively. Others are motivated to resist the meeting, the message, or the program. Some will resist quietly, sullenly or through nonparticipation. Other negative audience members choose to resist more actively, even more publicly, sabotaging through a wide variety of techniques such as being extra slow to enter the room or even quite late, standing in the back drinking coffee and whispering, ostentatiously reading newspapers or other material during the speech, asking irrelevant and/or irreverent questions of the speaker, and so on. Again, these people are quite motivated—just not in the hoped-for direction.

The speakers in these examples have to understand the main sets of motivations already existent in the groups in order to reach them in these admittedly difficult situations. If the speaker resorts to old homilies and what is sometimes called "the common wisdom" the presentation is probably doomed. Appeals to altruism will not always reach fertile ground. Assuming that everyone in the room is the same as everyone else is a guarantee of failure. The effective motivational speaker must learn about these motivations as they apply to all people in general and then, through research into this specific audience, how these motivations are at work among them.

The successful motivational speaker, having done his or her homework in terms of researching this particular audience, will speak to the various constituencies present in the group, making sure to be inclusive rather than exclusive. The main theme of the talk may be contrary to the wishes or upsetting to the sensitivities or desires of some subgroups, but to be successful, the speaker must at least bow toward those groups by acknowledging their concerns and showing them respect. In the best of cases, the motivational speaker will be able to suggest a synthesis in which the needs, views, and concerns of each major subgroup are shown to have common cause with the needs and concerns of the majority.

When the audience recognizes that you have gone out of your way to find out about them and tailor your speech directly to their concerns, their receptivity to you and your ideas is markedly increased. Too many audiences have heard the generic speech and the canned half-time talk, and they tend to resent having to sit through something so "same-old, same-old." Conversely, they are delighted and grateful when you have made the effort to aim your talk accurately, when it is clear that you have personalized and customized your presentation.

HUMAN MOTIVATIONS: THE SHORT LIST

Humans are motivated by a rather extensive list of concerns and needs. Because this is a book about motivational speaking and not a psychological or sociological text, we will

explore only a limited number of these motivations, but we
will focus on the most significant that can empower the
motivational speaker.

There are *physical* needs: water, food, shelter, and sex.
These needs usually (but not always) take precedence over
most others. The starving person doesn't think about his self-
esteem, for example. The parched person crawling under the
desert sun cannot discuss his achievements or the argument
he had last year with his supervisor. When an audience is
hungry or has been sitting too long, the motivational speaker
is fighting an uphill battle if he or she chooses to continue
with the talk. The audience is motivated to go to the snack
table, to the bathroom, and simply just move around. A successful motivational speaker doesn't fight the physical needs
of the audience. On the contrary, if possible, the motivational
speaker makes sure that the room's temperature is appropriate, the seats are as comfortable as possible, and the lighting
is just right for the type of presentation being offered. If it is
within the control of the speaker (and it can be—at least
partly—if you discuss these issues with your meeting planner
in advance), the events or speakers just preceding the motivational speech are kept short and positive, there is food and
drink available before the speech, and access to the bath-
rooms has been clearly available, too.

When I have had to present after a long and sometimes
boring introductory session (the CEO reads the sales statistics
in detail for 20 minutes followed by the company attorney
discussing the negative outcomes of two recent court cases!), I
have asked my host or meeting planner to give the audience
a short 10-minute stretch break before I am to be introduced.
Barring that, I've asked the audience to stand and stretch and
even conducted an organized and humorous stretch session
at the beginning of my presentation complete with music to
stretch by! (I've used contemporary hits such as the music to

the dance, *The Macarena,* or James Brown's famous *I Feel Good* song.) This activity actually starts the audience off in high energy and a positive mood, and it establishes your personal control over the group and its direction. People are grateful because they've had a chance to move and recuperate from such long inactivity.

There are many other possibilities for dealing with the audience's physical needs. For example, you could ask a key question—one that may lie at the core of your ensuing presentation—and then ask each member of your audience to pick a nearby partner and stand with his or her partner to discuss their own answers to that key question for two minutes. Make sure they are standing up in order to get some physical movement involved. At the end of that, you've gotten your audience awake and alive again as well as having cued them to be thinking about the main issues you're about to confront.

You could ask for several volunteers—I usually keep it to three or fewer—and ask them to answer a key question or be interviewed by you in the style of Oprah Winfrey (it helps to have a wireless hand microphone for this one) and then, based on the answers you receive, begin your talk in response to the audience's own input! I always reward my volunteers with something tangible such as an autographed copy of one of my books, a copy of some vital research that I've found on the issues important to this group, or a gag gift such as a red foam clown nose, a pair of Groucho glasses, or something else guaranteed to bring a smile.

The physiological need for shelter includes the need to be in a space that isn't too hot or cold or humid or dry. Try to motivate a group that's sweltering and falling asleep from the heat! I have had rooms that were broiling and ones that were freezing. These kinds of environments are really not conducive to any kind of speech, let alone a motivational one. That is one of the many reasons why I always discuss the meeting room well in advance with the meeting planner. And why I make sure that I arrive well before the start of my presentation.

Recently, I was speaking to a high school faculty in northern Illinois. When I arrived at the high school, I found the auditorium was just short of freezing. A recent heavy snowstorm was a major topic of conversation in the school. I asked the custodian to turn up the heat. Because he was working very hard that day, running from room to room helping with audio-visual equipment, he was rather overheated and had not noticed the temperature of the auditorium. "Oh, is it cold in here? OK, I'll do what I can." Had I not said anything, my audience would have sat there shivering while I tried to help them make a difference with their students. This sounds obvious, but it really isn't. Do whatever you can do to prevent human physical needs from being an issue in your presentation.

MASLOW'S HIERARCHY
OF HUMAN NEEDS

Abraham Maslow, one of the greatest and most noted psychologists of the 20th century, developed a list of basic human needs. He organized these needs into a *hierarchy.* He felt that certain needs took precedence over others. The physical needs began his list because, when unmet, they tended to block the individual from perceiving or responding to his other needs.

Second on Maslow's hierarchy was *safety,* the need to feel free from imminent danger. If people are convinced that they are in danger, they will not be able to consider almost anything else. One day, I was presenting a workshop at a major hotel in Honolulu. Suddenly, a loud noise and a puff of smoke came from the PA system amplifier. Smoke kept billowing out. Incredibly, the meeting planner signaled for me to just go on. The audience looked startled, and some seemed even frightened. I asked the audience to get up and leave the room in an orderly fashion. As they were doing so, the smoke alarms went off. As we all went out into the patio, the fire department arrived complete with sirens and men rushing around with hoses.

About an hour and a half later, they allowed us back into the room. Now cleared of smoke, the room slowly filled with my audience again. The hotel had brought in a new portable PA system. I began with a joke about the speaker's hot air triggering the smoke alarms, and the audience laughed. I then asked if everyone felt OK and safe enough for us to go on. Just asking that question seemed to calm the group because I was acknowledging publicly out loud their own concerns. Of course, I had ample opportunity for a series of groaners such as, "I'm here to fire you up," "We've really got some hot opportunities," and so on. I asked the audience to help me with the fire jokes, and you can bet they did. It was probably the most interactive keynote address I've ever done. How would that group have responded had I ignored their safety needs? Safety needs could not be ignored at that moment, nor can they be ignored when planning your pre-sentation. Safety needs also include needs for peacefulness, security, and lack of danger and threat.

Maslow then adds *belongingness* and *love*. People need affection, inclusion, caring, or relationship with others. When people's need for caring is not met, they can become highly motivated to move toward others. People need to feel they are a part of a family, group, or otherwise have a place, a sense of "at-home-ness." They want an identification with the group and its goals and accomplishments. They want to feel loved and worthy of love and affection, friendship, and loyalty. They want to feel connected to significant others. When people feel isolated, unloved or unliked, rejected or disincluded, they may become motivated either positively to seek inclusion or negatively to sulk, withdraw, and even seek revenge against those who rejected them. Some are motivated to seek inclusion or connectedness but have little or no skills to attain this goal. Their efforts may actually result in more rejection. So powerful are the needs for affection, inclusion, or love that people will often distort themselves out of all recognition in order to fit in or become accepted. No one wants to stand out like a sore thumb or be the isolate unlike anyone else and unliked by them. This desire to be included, to become part of something bigger than one's self, is one of the most potent needs that the motivational speaker can utilize in reaching a group. The motivational speaker can show how participants can become more accepted by the group or conduct an activity that helps people reduce their fear of rejection or an interactive activity that encourages people to get to know each other better, and this need for relationship and acceptance will feel more fulfilled.

At a recent teacher's conference, over 400 teachers from many widely separated buildings in a huge metropolitan countywide school system entered my room for a seminar on student motivation. I began, after the usual introductions, by showing several slides of my family, accompanied by proud and also humorous comments about each family member. Then I said, "OK, those are some of the pictures in *my* wallet, now is the time for you to show the pictures from *your* wallet or purse! If you don't have pictures with you, visualize the pictures you have at home, and get ready to talk about them." I directed each member of my audience to choose a partner sitting nearby—but not someone sitting immediately on the right or left (the ones they were most likely to already know) and take turns showing pictures and talking about the people in those pictures. I gave them three minutes. At the end of that time, I rang a gong to signal the end of the activity. People asked for more time! I extended it another few minutes. When the group quieted and I resumed my talk, there was a palpable difference in the feel of the group: They were more relaxed, more attentive, with smiles on their faces, and I could see no signs of that participant resistance that often marks teacher in-service audiences. As the seminar progressed, I asked participants to form small groups to discuss classroom issues and problems. The level of excited and fully committed participation was astoundingly high. Later the meeting planner remarked that she had never seen her colleagues really get into an in-service workshop so fully. The secret: An audience from widely scattered work sites needs to develop some sense of community of shared interests, feelings, and experiences in order to feel trust and lower their anxiety and to find reasons to risk sharing their ideas and problems. That wallet exercise was the key to helping them satisfy their need for connectedness, inclusion—to build a sense of shared community.

Other approaches to fulfilling this need might include (1) describing in your talk the unique and admirable qualities you found in the group, (2) the special and praiseworthy values the group is known for, or (3) its excellent reputation in the wider world. The audience members will tend to feel highly motivated because of their identification with the group. There is this one caveat: The unique qualities or excellent reputation have to be true. The audience will know very quickly if they are being manipulated, and this ploy will backfire. Make it clear how you know that these qualities are unique or that their reputation is so very fine.

After one's needs for inclusion are satisfied, the individual's *self-esteem needs* become predominant. Self-esteem encompasses ideas like self-respect, self-confidence, a sense of one's ability or competence. One of the best authors in the field of self-esteem is my colleague and friend, Dr. Nathaniel Branden. He terms the competence need as the need for *efficacy* or *agency*. People want to feel able to achieve and accomplish as well as feel that they are respected, admired, and valued for their contributions to the group. Personal recognition and prestige are aspects of this need for self-esteem.

Here the motivational speaker finds fertile territory. To publicly celebrate selected individuals for their achievement or contribution to the company, the school, the association, makes all members feel good. This can be especially powerful if the speaker can contrast the achievement of the group or company or school with comparable groups who have done less and then emphasize the contribution of this given individual to helping the group attain such a remarkable level of success.

There are several dangers in publicly celebrating selected individuals. First, the individuals may be embarrassed rather than delighted with the recognition. This can be due to their shyness, or occasionally the chosen individual truly does not share the perception of their excellence. The very shy individual can actually be demotivated by public praise. Whenever possible, try to ensure that this person is comfortable with public notice. Another pitfall is that people not chosen can feel resentment or envy. This can be exacerbated by the choice of only people from certain units while other units are ignored. Make sure, if you are selecting individuals for special mention, that you do so with help from knowledgeable members of the group so you can be certain to include someone from each unit or job category. One way to accomplish this is to conduct a very short "interview" (often just before the meeting begins, out near the refreshment table) in which you ask individuals what they are most proud of in their work or what their biggest accomplishments may be. Take notes afterward—a key phrase or short sentence will usually be enough to trigger your memory during your speech—and choose your individuals for special mention from among the people who give you the best answers to your question. By quoting them, there is an implied permission you receive because the comments you are making are those they felt good about sharing publicly with you. A variation of this is to ask your meeting planner to give you the names of six to eight "unsung heroes" in the group. Ask for photos of these people with a short paragraph outlining their special contributions to the group. Have those photos scanned and enlarged and printed out as transparencies or slides, or put them into your presentation program, and you have a dramatically personalized celebratory moment in your speech!

Maslow's list goes on to what he called the higher needs: *self-actualization*—moving toward the realization of one's potential—growing toward maturity, health, autonomy. Self-actualization needs can be difficult ones to address in a motivational talk because of their intangibility. Yet these strivings can represent important areas of personal growth and of emerging commitment for members of the audience. Trace an individual's growth from entry level to his or her current high level of achievement in the group, and, by implication, you'll be talking to everyone's need for growth and improvement. Describe the opportunity or career ladder that is or will be available in the company, and you're speaking to this need for advancement and ambition. Outline how a member of the group has been given an increasing level of autonomy in decision making, and you'll be talking directly to this need. Tell a story of how that person innovated, thought "outside of the box," or untangled a company traffic jam, and you have struck home to this need in your audience's hearts.

A wonderful way of doing this is to build your entire talk (or a major section of it) around a selected person or work team. Using the format of the old "This Is Your Life" TV show, you serve as an emcee, introducing ideas and then people who will rise from the audience (or come from behind the curtains) to describe in glowing terms some aspect of the individual's or group's progress toward their current achievement.

Maslow then tells us that people's *curiosity needs* come into play: the desire to know, to learn, to contribute knowledge. A talented motivational speaker might tell a story that is structured like a mystery. Dropping clues judiciously throughout the story, the speaker describes an actual person in the audience and that person's learning something of great value to the company, school, work team, or how he or she achieved a critical insight that enabled some target to be met. As the story progresses, the audience has the opportunity to guess the insight or the nugget of knowledge their colleague attained. It could even be done somewhat like a quiz show with the correct answer being found in a sealed envelope. Or the actual person involved has been asked to stand up at the penultimate moment, on your cue, to reveal the answer—and garner the group's applause as well. In one similar event, I had more than 500 envelopes, each with the correct answer enclosed, taped to the underside of every chair in the room. At the key moment, I revealed that, if they'd look under their chairs they'd find out "what Marvin discovered for your company!" I was later told that the fact sheets, enclosed in those envelopes, appeared on many, many cubicles, bulletin boards, and desktops. It was hard-earned knowledge, and Marvin's colleagues recognized its value. By having the sheet prominently titled, "Marvin Kaminsky's Marvelous Message" along with his mailstop, phone number, and e-mail address, Marvin received the credit he richly deserved, and everyone else got the message that their efforts at learning and adding to the company's store of useful knowledge would be recognized.

Then people have *aesthetic needs:* an interest in beauty, symmetry, rightness, perfection. Design a speech in which key concepts are arranged in a symmetrical pattern. Plan a part of a talk that focuses on the "just-rightness" of certain designs the company has produced, the perfect fit of the marketing plan with the segment of the marketplace that is the company's target for the product line. These strategies will help the audience see that their aesthetic needs can be satisfied by working here. Don't be afraid to talk about it. Intersperse your talk with artistic words and phrases: "He used his full *artistry* by . . . " or "Look at the *beauty* of how this remediation plan matched every point in the needs survey," or "See the *balance* between the elements of the new program." Don't be afraid to point out that we don't have to be artists in order to enjoy work that has artistic elements, color, light and dark, balance, harmony, positive tension and resolution, music, surprise, pattern, or repetition. Find these elements in your audience's work. Help them to see the artistry, the satisfying aesthetic elements in their endeavors, or build into your presentation opportunities for them to share them with you. Ask questions about these elements as you do your prepresentation interviews and research.

Finally, Maslow's hierarchy of human needs has as its pinnacle *transcendent* needs, which include altruism, a developing sense of the unity of all things, intuition, a sense of vision, and a view of the world beyond the narrow focus of one's ego. Point out how the group has been (or has the opportunity to be) charitable or responsive to local community needs or the needs of one's country. Hunt for these elements in examples drawn from your audience's life's work or from great exemplars in their professions.

Maslow's famous hierarchy of human needs has great value for the motivational speaker because it points out the areas in which we can reliably assume our audiences will have great interest. The motivational speaker will also find these additional areas of human need to be of value:

1. *Remind people of their original motivations,* which brought them to the job or profession they now occupy. Those who work at something a long time can lose their edge, their passion about their job. We can get very far removed

from the naive but powerful reasons we first entered the job. Bringing that back, in a tender and positive way, can restimulate those old feelings.

2. Touch the "heart space"—those higher values we learned from our parents and pastors such as love, conscience, altruism, generosity, sharing, sense of rightness. We have an inner voice that speaks to us, to some louder than to others, of what is right, of what is good. When we answer that inner voice, we do feel the best we can ever feel about ourselves. Reminding your audience—especially avoiding preachiness—of this voice can be a powerful tool for motivation.

3. *Sympathy, empathy, and identification* are really strong motivators. Sympathy is our tendency to feel similar feelings to feelings in others. When someone is crying, you may find tears coming to your own eyes. That is sympathy. Any feeling can engender sympathy; infectious laughter is another example. Empathy is somewhat different—it is when you understand and care about someone else's feelings without necessarily experiencing those feelings yourself. When you say, "Put yourself in this person's place," you are attempting to invoke empathy. Empathy allows us to predict what someone will feel in a given situation. Both of these are examples of the process of identification. If you tell your audience a story of a typical coworker having an unusual and moving experience, you are invoking identification.

    Tell your audience a story about your own experience, a moment in time when you had a strong feeling about some issue, problem, or concern that they share, or a situation in which you learned something the hard way, and your audience is likely to identify with you and get the point memorably.

4. *Religion, belief, and spirituality* constitute one of the most powerful motivators available—and one of the most fraught with danger for the speaker. People's religious feelings are complex and fervent. The motivational speaker has to use uncommon sense and tread very carefully in this area. Do you know, for certain, what religious beliefs

are held by the members of your audience? Are there many religious denominations represented in your audience? Are there important areas of agreement that cross religious boundaries and can be the ones you touch upon? Religious feelings are potent because they represent the individual's desire to find meaning in his or her life; because they were taught by one's parents and/or culture; and because they may represent the hope for a future afterlife, redemption. Yet religious values also are the underpinning of every society, the basis of ethics and morals, the source of that inner voice of which we spoke earlier. Use this profound source of motivation, but do so with care, with respect for members of the group who may not share the majority's version of religion.

5. *Achievement, pride, and feelings of competence* are motivations present in everyone—the desire to achieve meaningful accomplishments, to feel pride in one's endeavors, to feel competent or able. They exist in all area's of one's life—from the desire to achieve good relationships with one's spouse, parents, and children, to the desire to do well at work, be able to be equal with one's coworkers in contribution to the group's success. Fill your speech with specific, accurate, and dramatic examples of the achievements of the group or its members, and your audience will feel motivated. Build into your talk an opportunity for members of the audience to share a success with someone seated nearby, and you'll anchor this powerful motivation with recent positive experience.

6. *Anger, hurt, resentment, and the need for revenge* are the darker side of the human spirit but potent motivations nonetheless. It would be irresponsible and reckless to directly utilize these motivations in a speech unless one is attempting to calm these feelings or provide a positive or creative way for the group to cope with them or resolve them. Here is where the motivational speaker can talk about the redemptive and healing power of forgiveness and how holding on to anger and resentment steals one's own energy and distracts us from using our talents most effectively. Two of the most effective motivational speak-

ers on this topic are Dr. Sidney Simon and Suzanne Simon, whose book *Forgiveness* remains a classic "must-read" on this topic. They have helped many groups to transcend impacted negative feelings to reach new levels of growth and achievement as well as rediscovering their energy to create and produce their own best work once they've abandoned the need for revenge and ceased carrying the heavy baggage of unresolved anger.

7. *Competitiveness and the desire for excellence* can be compelling motivations for most people—except those who have already given up, who see no hope for themselves, or believe the adversary is too powerful to overcome. Most people, at least in our society, seem to have feelings of competitiveness. We have the tendency to compare ourselves to others, to published standards, or to our own past levels of achievement. Our fascination with sports keeps this aspect of our lives stirred up and always somewhere near the surface. Closely related to competitiveness is our desire for excellence, our need to become more than merely adequate at what we do. All of human endeavor offers reinforcement for this desire: awards, prizes, standards, seals of approval, tests of significance as well as symbols such as Olympic gold medals, *The Guinness Book of World Records*. Show your audience the path to excellence, and then challenge them to take it.

8. *Fear and the need to resolve it* are another way of expressing what Maslow called the *safety* need. You can remind your audience of the dangers they are in or might someday be in and point out how they can conquer those dangers through preparation or commitment. This is, again, one of the darker motivational forces and, as such, brings with it those dangers we've discussed. When reminding people about dangers, you run big risks of demotivating them, of restimulating their fears to the point of their decision to take no action, withdraw, or become depressed or phobic. Many people, faced with continuous or overwhelming threat, return to old, safe areas of behavior. Even though those behaviors may have absolutely nothing to do with solving their current problems, this retreat helps them

feel safer. Triggering such a retreat is not what you want to accomplish. If, however, the fears are already there and topmost on people's minds, then confronting those fears and offering a path toward their resolution makes a great deal of sense. The stock prices have fallen dramatically because a new competitor's product line is vastly out-selling yours. The board of directors is calling for cost-cutting measures, and several big stockholders have just filed suit. The whole company stands at the brink. To ignore this would be foolish. Yet, if there were easy, obvious answers, they would have been done already. Your challenge in that situation is to begin with the facts, tough as they are, and point out the available options. If you are the consultant who has helped the company's directors or management choose their new strategy, you can outline that for your audience. More likely, you are the motivational speaker whose job it is to sell that new strategy to the group. You've got to marshal all the facts and the reasons why the new strategy is likely to succeed—if the whole company gets behind it. At such a moment, mentioning their fears and the problems faced by the company is the most appropriate thing to do. You will have a very attentive audience as you get to the part where the new strategy is outlined!

9. *Adventure, excitement, change, risk, and danger* can be powerful motivators. When people are bored because they've been doing the same things for a very long time, or because they're at the top and there seem to be no new mountains to climb, they begin to crave adventure, excitement, and change. I believe that there are three levels at which most people operate: *the survival level,* where they are using almost all their energy just to get through the day's challenges alive; *the maintenance level,* where they use a middling level of energy to survive and have some energy left over to repair or plan for repairing things that have gone wrong or decide how to prevent problems from occurring; and *the enhancement level,* in which they begin to actively seek new challenges or plan entirely new programs, design new products and programs, learn new

skills. You can utilize this desire to grow, or as they used
to say in the "Star Trek" series, "to boldly go where no
one has gone before." This motivation works only when
the majority of your audience is really at that place.
Although there are always some few individuals who are
unable to reach this level, there are many times when
most of the group is really craving a change, a chance to
be different, an opportunity to test themselves against the
new mountain. If you misread the group, however, and
most of them are down at the survival or maintenance
levels, they will look at you either blankly or with gen-
uine hostility when you exhort them to gear up for climbing that new peak.

10. *Use humor, fun, playfulness, and lightness.* The human ani-
mal likes to laugh. We simply cannot be serious all the
time. There is a need to lighten things up at all times, but
when the situation is perilous or tense, the need for
humor can become very strong. By interspersing well-chosen humor in your presentation, you utilize this need as
one of the engines to propel your motivational message.
Even more powerfully, you can find humorous examples
from the recent history of your host group or involve
your audience in humorous activities or strategies. One of
the most effective humorous speakers is Dr. Matt Weinstein, whose company, Playfair, has an international reputation for bringing humor into the business world. His
book, *Managing to Have Fun,* is an inspiring and eye-opening primer on how humor can create the kind of workplace that keeps people highly motivated and productive.
His colleague (and coauthor on another wonderful book,
Playfair) Dr. Joel Goodman says, "Take your job seriously
and yourself lightly." Both of these exciting motivational
speakers have learned to utilize this powerful human need
to reach audiences around the world.

Humor works to lower anxiety, release tension, and
reduce the psychological distance between people. Once
you've laughed with someone, it is harder to be alienated
from him or her. Humor can make others seem more

approachable and sympathetic. It is critically important that humor be positive and not bitter, discriminatory, racist, sexist, or otherwise involving put-downs and the diminishment of others. This is not put here for political correctness but for effectiveness. Because of rising sensitivities, it is harder today to use humor that the entire audience will buy into without controversy. People who go to comedy clubs or watch late-night comedy cable networks may be ready to accept humor with blue language and jokes that trash particular groups—often told by members of the same group! But people in a company, school, or organization's meeting will not accept such humor passively. Instead of motivating your audience, such humor undoes any power the rest of your message may have had. Find humor that, if it pokes fun, does so gently. Humor that lasts is the kind that releases the tensions in human situations that we all have experienced—humor that finds the situation funny, that reminds us when we've gotten too caught up in our own egos.

USING THE HUMAN MOTIVATIONS

These are the human motivations you can tap as a motivational speaker. This list is intended to begin your search for your own keys to human motivations. As you plan your presentation, ask yourself these questions:

1. What human needs, motives, desires, or concerns are at work in my intended audience? How do I know that? How can I confirm that?
2. What needs or concerns are implied by my topic or by the situation in which my audience members find themselves?
3. Are there subgroups that have special concerns or needs that must be acknowledged in my presentation?
4. What do I know (or can I find out) that can help this audience move toward the satisfaction of those needs?

5. What experiences do I have with similar situations or similar motivations in my own life that I can use as examples and use to help myself empathize with my audience?

BIBLIOGRAPHY

Blakely, James, *et al. How the Platform Professionals Keep 'Em Laughin'.* Houston, TX: Rich Publishing Co., 1987.

Blumenfeld, Esther, and Lynne Alpern. *The Smile Connection: How to Use Humor in Dealing with People.* New York: Prentice-Hall, 1986.

Garland, Ron. *Making Work Fun: Doing Business with a Sense of Humor.* San Diego, CA: Shamrock Press, 1991.

Green, Lila. *Making Sense of Humor: How to Add Joy to Your Life.* Manchester, CT: KIT Publisher, 1993.

Kushner, Malcolm. *The Light Touch: How to Use Humor for Business Success.* New York: Simon and Schuster, 1990.

Metcalf, C. W., and Roma Felible. *Lighten Up: Survival Skills for People Under Pressure.* Reading, MA: Addison-Wesley, 1992.

Robertson, Jeanne. *Humor: The Magic of Genie.* Houston, TX: Rich Publishing, 1990.

Seligman, Martin E. P. *Learned Optimism: How to Change Your Mind and Your Life.* New York: Simon and Schuster, 1990.

Simon, Sidney B., and Suzanne Simon. *Forgiveness: How to Make Peace with Your Past and Get on with Your Life.* New York: Warner Books, 1991.

Weinstein, Matt. *Managing to Have Fun: How Fun at Work Can Motivate Your Employees.* New York: Simon and Schuster, 1996.

Weinstein, Matthew, and Joel Goodman. *Playfair: Everybody's Guide to Non-Competitive Play.* San Luis Obispo, CA: Impact Publishers, 1986.

Wilson, Steve. *The Art of Mixing Work and Play.* Columbus, OH: Applied Humor Systems, Inc., 1992.

WHAT IS A MOTIVATIONAL SPEECH?

A MOTIVATIONAL SPEECH AS A RELATIONSHIP

The Famous Speaker

I have been very fortunate to be in the audience at many incredibly motivating speeches. I've heard Matthew Weinstein, Anthony Robbins, Jack Canfield, Mark Victor Hansen, Carl Boyd, John Alston, Zig Ziglar, Jeannie Robertson, and many others. Something happens at a motivational speech: An electricity is in the air. When the speaker is well-known, that electricity precedes the speaker. The audience is warmed up simply by their expectation of the speaker's greatness. The introducer's job is easy because the audience already believes that this is going to be a memorable experience. The welcoming applause dies down, and the speaker pauses for effect. When the speaker begins, the crowd is totally hushed, drinking in every word and gesture. Perhaps something dramatic occurs that the audience is already expecting, a "signature" piece of stage business that grabs attention or gets a laugh. The event has begun. People are congratulating themselves for being there.

The Less Well-Known Speaker

When the speaker is relatively or completely unknown to the audience, there may be more noise in the room and less attentiveness as the introducer begins. In fact, people may be uncertain as to what's going to happen, wondering if it is worthwhile being here for this event. The speaker's beginning may be up against crowd noise, talking, rustling of papers. If the speaker is experienced and/or talented, something happens in the first three to five minutes to grab the audience, gain control of the room. The speaker does something dramatic or funny or touching. Suddenly you can hear a pin drop during every pause in the speech. The audience has surrendered to the experience. It's a motivational speech. People are now ready to be motivated. In fact, I think that there's a little dance, a structured interaction that is probably cultural in nature. The group has some expectations about what a good speaker is going to do and how he or she is going to be. The audience actually wants to be motivated, captivated, seduced (if you will) by the presentation. They'd love to surrender to the moment, to the experience. They hunger to believe again in the program, the job, the group, the company, the profession, or whatever the speech is to be about. No one really loves being burnt out or cynical or sarcastic or depressed, tuned out, and apathetic. It is much more fun, one feels much more alive, when one believes in what one is doing. If the speaker can only tap into this, the moment is made. The people will come alive again. They will be grateful to the speaker, grateful to the meeting planner, and delighted with themselves for being able to believe again!

CHARACTERISTICS OF A MOTIVATIONAL SPEECH

Every speech should be motivational in that the speaker should have presented important, relevant, and fresh information in a way that piques the audience's interest and leaves them wanting to remember the information and use it in their personal or professional lives. Having said that, I must admit that many speeches I've heard failed to match that model, but, from the point of view of the audience, they certainly wished the speeches did! The audience, you see, is really on your side. They don't want to be bored or disappointed. They would much rather that you succeed. They'd love it if today's speech is fun, fast-paced. and fascinating.

The speech that is labeled as "motivational," and that was designed or intended to be motivational has certain unique characteristics that differentiate it from speeches that were intended to be merely entertaining or humorous or perhaps informational and even skill-building.

The Need for Inspiration

The motivational speech should have the quality of *inspiration,* of presenting information, ideas, themes, concepts, or information with the goal of increasing the listener's motivation, which I define as *the desire and intention to do particular things, achieve certain goals, take on specific attitudes, begin desired processes and procedures.* Motivational speeches differ from all others in that they are *deliberately designed to induce motivation.* Other speeches may be *incidentally* motivating, but the motivational speech is so by design and intent.

An informative speech can be motivational because people do feel more positively disposed toward topics about which they feel they have enough information to be confident and comfortable. If the information they receive has the character of being shocking, unexpected, or frightening or implies some problem that needs resolution, the audience can be motivated even if the speaker fails to draw the moral and urge action. Speaking to a group of parents and letting

them know about planned cuts in funding for a valued read-
ing-enhancement program may produce strong and even
unintended motivation.

A speech designed to help build skills—for example, a talk
about the most effective techniques of cold-calling for salespeople—may produce motivation in a sales group, because as
they feel more likely to succeed at a strategy, they will be
more willing and even eager to try out the techniques mentioned in the talk. Many kinds of speeches can have as a col-
lateral or side effect the motivation of the audience. But only
the motivational speech has been deliberately and knowingly
planned to have this effect.

Motivational speeches do not have only one possible format or only a limited number of styles and techniques. It is
possible to design a motivational speech that uses as its main
propulsive force humor, personal stories, shocking facts and
exposés, or appeals to patriotism, loyalty, friendship, or any
number of things. The essence of the motivational speech is
in its intended outcome: human motivation. *If the speech is a
catalyst for a commitment by the audience toward the desired
goals, it is motivational, whatever its content, style, or technique.*

Your Own Belief Is the Key

In ancient Rome, a respected senator from an old and powerful patrician family, Cato the Elder, rose to speak in the Senate
one day, as was his right and privilege. When he was recognized by the Speaker, he simply said, *"Cartago delenda est!"*
[Carthage must be destroyed!] and promptly sat down, to the
consternation and confusion of the other senators. Some tit-
tered, others muttered in derision. At that time, Carthage was
a trading partner and competitor of Rome but certainly not its
enemy. In fact, many Roman families had important financial
ties and business interests in Carthage. When he was asked to

explain, Cato the Elder said nothing. His remarks were dismissed as an aberration. The next day, Cato rose again and demanded the floor. Again, when recognized, in ringing tones he declared, *"Cartago delenda est!"* Again, there were derisive whispers and a few laughs. Most did not want to offend his powerful family and remained silent. But the Senate went on with its business without further comment.

Every day, for nearly three years, Cato rose and spoke his famous line, *"Cartago delenda est!"* At first, it was met with incredulity. After a while, it was met with open hostility and derision. Taunting, teasing, loud hostile commentary became the norm—for a while. But the power of Cato's consistency, of his steadfastness in the face of ridicule, of the certitude with which he spoke, began to erode the opposition. Gradually, almost imperceptibly, senators began to view news of Carthage with suspicion. Otherwise ordinary events were now viewed through a new lens and interpreted as possible support for Cato's position. Almost three years later, the Roman Senate unanimously voted to declare war on Carthage. In the war that ensued, Carthage was indeed destroyed, and Rome's main competitor in the Mediterranean was no more. Rome gained immeasurably from this conflict, started by one man, with one simple insistent message. That is the power of a motivational speech. In this case, its length was unimportant, he did not use an overhead projector, a computerized presentation program, or a service bureau to process his slides. His most powerful techniques were repetition and his own unshakable belief in his idea. That belief was translated into his tone of voice, his volume, his nonverbal behavior as he looked majestically around the senate chamber, delivering his one-line peroration.

More recent history is replete with examples of leaders giving motivational addresses with stunning power, often in wartime. Lincoln's famed Gettysburg Address galvanized a nation reeling from one of the most disastrous "victories" possible. Yes, the Union carried the day at Gettysburg, but at the cost of many thousands dead and wounded. How to repair the fighting spirit of that nation? Following a famous speaker, Edward Everett, who spoke for nearly two and a half hours (the audiences of that day had far more sticking power than those of today), Lincoln gave his message in 271 words.*

Fourscore and seven years ago our fathers brought forth upon this continent, a new nation, conceived in Liberty, and dedicated to the proposition that all men are created equal.

Now we are engaged in a great civil war, testing whether that nation, or any nation so conceived, and so dedicated, can long endure. We are met on a great battle-field of that war. We have come to dedicate a portion of that field, as a final resting place for those who here gave their lives, that that nation might live. It is altogether fitting and proper that we should do this.

But, in a larger sense, we can not dedicate—we can not consecrate—we can not hallow—this ground. The brave men, living and dead, who struggled here, have consecrated it, far above our poor power to add or detract. The world will little note, nor long remember, what we say here, but it can never forget what they did here. It is for us the living, rather, to be dedicated here to the unfinished work which they who fought here, have, thus far, so nobly advanced. It is rather for us to be here dedicated to the great task remaining before us—that from these honored dead we take increased devotion to that cause for which they here gave the last full measure of devotion—that we here highly resolve that these dead shall not have died in vain—that this nation, under God, shall have a new birth of freedom—

---

*Lincoln wrote out his Gettysburg Address six times, all apparently with slight differences. This version is from one of the five existing handwritten copies, which is displayed at the Old State Capitol in Springfield, Illinois.

and that, government of the people, by the people, for the people, shall not perish from the earth.

It is worth noting that many of the newspaper reporters present did not think much of the speech and focused most of their attention and dispatches on Everett's longer and more florid oratory. However, Everett himself, an extremely famous speaker of the day, immediately said that he wished he had given Lincoln's speech. He recognized the greatness in it despite (or maybe partly because of) its brevity.

MOTIVATION IS A COOPERATIVE VENTURE

A motivational speech does not gain its power by imposing new motivations upon its hearers. It is not likely that a speaker can singly imbue an audience with motivations with which they did not enter the room. Instead a motivational speaker attempts to uncover, understand, and tap into the motivations already present in the audience. Many years ago, in describing children's learning, educators used to say the child's mind was a *tabula rasa,* a blank slate, upon which the teacher writes the lesson. This presumed that children entered school totally blank, empty, devoid of knowledge, skills, preferences, abilities, disabilities, and prejudices. This view of learning seemed to give the teacher even more enormous power than he or she already has. The teacher supplied all knowledge, all skill, and imbued the child with all of his or her attitudes and beliefs about the subject and about him- or herself that would enable the child to use that knowledge constructively.

Reality is quite different from this now discredited view of learning. Children do not enter the schoolroom like blank tapes waiting to be recorded. Instead, by the time a child enters kindergarten, he or she has learned (in most cases) to walk, talk, sing, run, play, and perform many complicated maneuvers like working a VCR, playing with a computer, and so on. The child already has tastes ("I hate brussels sprouts!") and abilities ("I can get on the Internet and find the Disney Web page!") as well as learned helplessness in certain areas ("My Mom says she can't do math either!") and prejudices ("My dad says it's stupid for boys to have to take home economics!").

Similarly, your audience will walk into the room filled with their own life experiences, their own points of view, and systems of values. Before you begin your talk, they may have brought in anger ("The boss said we had to come to this #&^**@%!! meeting or else!") or fear ("I hear they're downsizing the company again. I wonder who gets the ax next?") They will be energized or exhausted, nervous or relaxed, hopeful or hopeless, elated or depressed, hungry or sated—all with no regard to you and your plans for them.

Will your talk really speak to them? Will it touch some resonant chord in their hearts? It will not do that as a result of your telling them how to feel or how to behave. It can only work if you've done your homework and discovered who they are, what issues are on their minds, what history has helped them feel that way, and what directions seem to make most sense to them.

Motivation is, therefore, not something one does *to* someone, but rather it is something one does *with* them. It is a cooperative venture. People resent being manipulated without their consent. They don't want to be psyched, hypnotized, controlled, dominated, or exploited. They will respond to those attempts with resistance, cynicism, anger, resentment, and hostility. Naked manipulation will rebound and produce the exact opposite to the desired outcome: a group not only not motivated in the direction you've chosen but angry and suspicious of you and whomever hired you to speak.

Motivation is a cooperative venture! It is your business to discover your audience's motivations and their desired goals. If you (or your hosts) think their goals are erroneously chosen or need revision, it is necessary for you to build that case for them and involve them cooperatively in seeing the new outcomes you think have more merit. When you touch upon their feelings and fears, their hopes and hurts, their experiences and expectations, do so tenderly and respectfully. Make yourself equally vulnerable to them by sharing your own hopes and dreams, your own similar or extraordinary experiences and the processes by which you came to the conclusions you will share with them.

LIGHT YOUR INNER FIRE
IN ORDER TO LIGHT THEIRS

Remember that the audience *wants* to be motivated. They want to be enthralled. They will be grateful to you if you can remind them of why they are there, of how they can restore their old feelings of motivation if those are now lost or faded. They will be delighted if you can restimulate in them an uncritical, unself-conscious, almost naïve faith in what they are doing, or what they ought to do, or what they are about to do. They will be relieved if you can help them find pride in their own selves, accomplishments, or actions for we live in an age of cynicism and self-consciousness. In our busy lives we rush around doing and doing. Sometimes the activity seems to take the place of thought. We may find no time or place for introspection, for thinking through the tough issues or for choosing thoughtfully our life's direction. The motivational speaker who is most successful is one who can nudge us in that direction or who can remind us of the need to take that moment to choose our next steps more wisely. A poster I have in my office says it best: *A friend is someone who knows your song and sings it to you when you forget.*

Whatever historians may decide about the greatness or ultimate value of John F. Kennedy's presidency, almost all agree that he was a consummately charismatic speaker. His inaugural address touched the hearts of so many of his fellow citizens: ". . . ask not what your country can do for you; ask what you can do for your country." Whatever he accomplished in his brief and fatally interrupted presidency, he managed to sing America's song back to us when it seemed that many had forgotten it. Thousands clamored to join the Peace Corps or engage in other public-spirited works as a result of that single famous motivational address. Want to be a motivational speaker? Find out what your audience's song is, and sing it to them, unashamedly, with spirit and conviction, with flamboyance, and with your own inner fire. Make yourself equally vulnerable by sharing how much of that song is yours, too, and you will have become a motivational speaker!

After that, all you need is practice and polish to become a professional motivational speaker. But without that singing of the audience's song, you cannot do the job, no matter how much polish you acquire.

5 PREPARING YOURSELF TO MOTIVATE OTHERS

The tip of the iceberg is the day you are standing up, poised, confident, smiling, just about to speak to the group. Looking wonderful, feeling ready, you and the group are expecting a wonderful experience. But how did you get there? It wasn't magic, and you didn't simply get up to give a speech spontaneously, without preparation. Like an Olympic ice skater who makes pirouettes and leaps look so easy, there are many steps to be taken and practiced before you are ready to perform.

There are many steps to take toward being fully prepared on the day you give your motivational speech. Most of these will take place in the weeks and then days before the actual talk. Finally, you will have much to do the night before the presentation and on the day of the presentation itself. The goal is to make the presentation seem effortless, artless, spontaneous, and heartfelt. To get there, you must begin a journey.

The negotiation is over; you've been chosen or hired to give a motivational address to a group. You've written or prepared the speech. It may be that you'll revise it before you deliver it, but as of now it is ready. If you are going to be able to motivate others, you have to deal with a myriad of details and dispose of them satisfactorily so they do not sap your energy or distract you from giving the best presentation possible.

THE WEEKS BEFORE THE PRESENTATION

Continuing Contact with Your Meeting Planner

It is important to stay in continuous contact with your meeting planner in the period from the time you are invited to speak until the actual presentation. Several phone calls are in order—to keep yourself and your meeting planner informed. Changes can and often do occur: The group may revise its schedule of presentations several times. They may change the timing, length, or *even the actual title or subject of your presentation* without consulting you. As odd as this may sound, it has happened to me and to a number of professional speakers of my acquaintance enough times to be worthy of your concern. The person assigned as your contact in the group may leave, be replaced, or otherwise become unavailable. Stay in touch with the group. You will be surprised to discover how much you will learn about the group with each call. These subtle learnings will positively affect the preparation of your speech.

In continuous contact, you will share your travel arrangements, including the name of the person who will pick you up at the airport (if you are flying) and how and when you will meet your contact person. You will have the opportunity to go over the room setup details and hear any last-minute concerns the group may have. Make sure you have phone numbers for emergencies. It helps to have your meeting planner's home phone number.

Final Preparations: The Week Before

Now is the time for a review of your speech. Do you have it internalized? Are you clear about the major points you will make? Are your notes ready? Do you need to make last-minute changes to your slides, transparencies, or computer presentation?

A checklist is always helpful. Add your own personal items to this one:

1. Copy of your speech
   a. What form will it take? A typescript, word-for-word; an outline of key points; a set of index cards with key points and quotes; or some other form?
2. Copies of your notes, note cards, "cheat sheet," or other memory aids
3. Slides or transparencies arranged properly, in order
4. Props
5. Handouts
   a. Will you carry them with you or send them, in advance, to your meeting planner?
6. Technology
   a. Wireless microphone (highly recommended)
   b. Laptop computer and display panel
   c. Slide projector/carousels
   d. Cassette recorder/CD player
   e. Cassettes or CDs chosen for this presentation
   f. Laser pointer
   g. Musical signal (I use a small tuning gong to gain the audience's attention when I give them an opportunity to speak with a partner)
7. Clothing to wear for the presentation
8. Interview data to be reviewed looking for "hot buttons" to remember during the speech

Make your own checklist based on the needs you have and the format and content of your talk. But a checklist is invaluable because of the stress associated with the imminent public appearance and the travel to it. At such moments, you do not want to arrive at your meeting location and suddenly become aware of the three important items you forgot.

THE NIGHT BEFORE THE PRESENTATION

Just as you have done your homework prior to the presentation, back in your office, through your research, your contact with the meeting planner, your prepresentation questionnaire (see Figure 2.1 beginning on page 24), your writing the speech and/or preparing your slides or presentation program, you should think of the night before the speech as an essential part of the preparation as well. You can help ensure success by using this evening effectively.

Choosing Clothes

It's time to choose your "presentation costume." Instead of thinking, "clothes," I use the word "costume" to describe this outfit. Cast yourself in the drama of your presentation. Are you playing the hero or heroine? Will you be admired, looked up to, respected? Who is this audience, and to what sort of person will they most respond? The costume you choose establishes your character as soon as you walk out upon the stage. A mentor of mine, Jean Wasserman, years ago gave me her rules for dressing for success: *"For a workshop, dress like the best-dressed member of your audience; for a keynote, dress one or two rungs above the best-dressed of your audience."* Over the years, I've found this advice to be remarkably accurate. In a workshop setting, the audience wants to respect you but feel close to you because you seem to be just like them in some important ways. In a keynote, the audience wants to look up to you, to see you as wrapped in an aura—it is, after all, a performance, a bit of show biz. They want you to glitter, to be elevated. One of the most effective motivational speakers I've ever known, one of my coauthors on *A 4th Course of Chicken Soup for the Soul,* Mark Victor Hansen, dresses incredibly well. His suits are the latest and best cuts. What really stand out are his ties. He invests time, energy, and cutting-edge taste (as well as considerable money) on picking spectacular ties. They aren't tacky, but they are really "out there." When you see his tie, you know this is a special man. That sets you up to listen, and, when you do, you are never disappointed, for as dramatic as the ties are, he is even more so, dispensing his unique brand of joy, infinite possibility, commitment to learning, overcoming, growing. He has been a mentor to me on this and many other issues for years.

Ask yourself, "Is my choice of clothing consistent with my intention, my message, the group, and its values?" If the answer is "yes," you've chosen well. Now, lay out the clothes carefully so that you won't have to worry or be flustered in the morning—or whenever you'll dress for the speech.

Packing Your Case

Do you have a carrying case in which to put all the basics you have ready for your presentation? A good case can be very handy for the motivational speaker. In here will go your speech, notes, props, wireless microphone, airline tickets, directions, and so on. The day or night before the presentation (or your travel to the presentation), you will want to pack this case carefully. Go over your checklist to make sure you have everything with you that you'll need. If you are traveling, you'll want to put any prescription medicines in it (so that, if you are separated from your luggage, at least the most important items are with you in your carry-on). I recommend that certain items become standards that are always in your carry-on case. Items such as a toiletries kit, some batteries (for your electronics), certain props you always use, certain intro slides you always use, blank transparencies and transparency markers, cables, extension cords, or whatever you know that you'll always want to have. If you have to always remember to pack these things, you will someday find yourself 500 miles from home without them.

Getting Enough Rest

As obvious as it might seem, you need to get enough rest the night before you present. Nervousness, the stress of travel, and the obligations of being social may intrude on this. You've landed in a city 2,000 miles from home. Your host picks you up at the airport and drives you to the hotel. At the hotel, seven members of the planning committee are waiting to take you to dinner. You are the out-of-town expert, and they are all excited to have the opportunity to be with you, hear you, and speak with you before everyone else will tomorrow. They are happy, elated, excited, and want to talk and talk. The dinner lasts until 10:30. They go home, and you are sitting on your bed in the hotel room, exhausted yet overstimulated. And, because of the late hour, you haven't had the chance to do that one last once-over of your speech and your slides that you had planned. Should you stay up and do it or turn out the lights and try to get some sleep? Tough choice. Perhaps you ought to have told your host in advance, "You know, when I arrive, if you and your committee would like to have dinner, I will be delighted! There's just one thing: I do need to get some rest prior to my talk, so can we arrange to be done with dinner by 9 P.M.?" By setting those boundaries early, you avoid unpleasant situations, and you also avoid being wrung out the morning of your talk.

Do you have some secret strategy for getting to sleep, especially when you are over tired or over stimulated? If you do, now is the time to deploy it. I find that a racing mind often stops me from sleeping. I am filled with ideas I don't want to forget the next day. So I take the little pad and pen that hotels keep by the phone and put it on the night stand.

I sit for a few minutes thinking about the next day. I mentally review my slides, my talk, my props. At such moments, lots of my concerns and ideas come up for me. I take notes and, by doing so, reassure myself that I won't forget them the next day. I find that very calming. I have also found that many hotel rooms are too bright—even with the lights off and the drapes drawn. So I carry a sleep mask for just such occasions. And I've found that foam earplugs, available at most pharmacies, will help if your room is located near noisy guests, a slamming elevator door, or the like.

I further cut down on worries that might keep me awake by bringing my own travel alarm—even though I will leave a request for a wake-up call with the front desk. I have had too many experiences with lost, forgotten, or mistaken wake-up calls that never came.

Watch Your Food Intake

On the road, there's a dangerous mental attitude that your normal diet is suspended during travel. Most of us learn, over time, what our body's favorite and unfavorite foods are. Often our mind likes one food that our digestive system doesn't like at all. Do you know which foods are likely to keep you up at night? It sounds silly to have to remind you, but most people sitting up at 3 A.M. are folks who really knew enough not to eat what they chose to eat anyway! Be aware of your diet at that convivial dinner with the committee.

The night before your presentation is usually not the best time to watch a lot of television—especially the late news, since those things tend to keep you up longer and later, and often the news is unsettling. I *do* like to watch the early evening news or the morning news while I am dressing, since those can give me local news items that may be important or useful to my talk. Many times I've heard something that can give me a humorous or topical lead-in to some part of my presentation.

I do believe in doing a run-through or review of the talk the night before. It can be very helpful and even reassuring to do so. However, avoid the trap of too many run-throughs. You can over practice and take the spontaneity out of it. Too many practices can also raise your anxiety because they are often a symptom of perfectionism. After one review, turn off the lights, and hit the bed. You'll need that energy tomorrow!

That Final Review

During that final review, I often have lots of ideas that I wish I'd had back at my office when I could have made a slide to insert into the talk or otherwise prepared material to illustrate or enrich that idea. (Ah, modern technology! If your talk is on your laptop and incorporated in a presentation program, you can instantly change, edit, or add to your presentation. Because I favor actual transparencies, I carry my laptop, a wonderful miniaturized color printer, and blank transparencies for just these events.) However, I really recommend that you try to cut items out of your talk rather than add to it. In our urge to help others (you are, after all, a motivational speaker!) and our desire to be perfect or at least seem so, we may have the tendency to want to add just one more fact, just one more example or story. There is a problem with overkill and with going over your allotted time. I promise you, very few speakers end their talks significantly earlier than scheduled. Most have a continual struggle with keeping within the time limits. Use that final review to tighten your talk, not expand it. Cut, cut, and cut again. Of course you should have done this back at the office, but you've got new insights now when the crunch is upon you. The pressure of the night before helps focus the mind in wonderful ways!

Three Plus Two

I follow a guideline that, in a motivational talk, people can cope with three major ideas and two additional "enrichment" or explication ideas. Now this is not a rule, merely a guideline. But if your talk really has 20 ideas in it, no matter how excellent your delivery, you will be putting some of your audience into a trance. The best talks are succinct. I confess that it's a constant struggle for me to obey my own guideline! Yet, whenever I've come closest to this ideal, those talks were the most successful and memorable, and I've felt the most pride in them.

THE DAY OF THE PRESENTATION

Motivating others can be a difficult proposition if you, yourself, are not motivated. With all the stressors that affect us today, it is very possible that you can find yourself about to give a motivational address and you are over tired, out of sorts, in a bad mood, or even filled with self-doubt. Your audience will sense your mood rather quickly, so it is imperative that you work on your own self to create and maintain a high level of mental preparation for this talk.

Centering Yourself

Lots of outside influences can cause us to lose sight of our goals, intentions, self-confidence, and inner vision. The hassle of traveling to the presentation, for example, can tire you out, disorient you, and raise your anger or anxiety. Unhelpful personnel at the conference site, lost materials, a room that isn't set up correctly, last-minute changes in the program can all conspire to leave you much less than at your best. It helps, therefore, to take some time, on the day of the presentation, to *center yourself*. That may seem to be a new-age term, but it is actually quite useful. Think of those moments in your life when you seem to be really functioning at top form. Your energy is high, your sense of purpose is clear, you feel in command of things, and even interruptions and problems do not seem to diminish your effectiveness. At the end of those moments, you look back on your work and you know that you've been completely congruent with your values, you have no regrets, you even feel pride in a job well done. Let us define that condition as "being centered." The values, beliefs, and hard-won skills that are at the core or center of your being have been enacted fully.

Do you want to give today's presentation that same quality? It is helpful for you to spend a little time and energy putting the distractions aside and focusing on that feeling of centeredness in order to reach it one more time. As you rise on the morning of the talk, think of your intentions today. What do you want to accomplish? What kind of person do you want to be today? What do you hope to bring to your audience today? Starting your day with that set of positive intentions clearly in mind will definitely help you focus your energy to attain those goals.

I begin each day with a simple phrase which I use to remind myself of my full intention: "This is it!" I remind myself, "Twenty years from now I will be going to the drug store more often. Today will become the good old days someday that I'll be looking back on with fond nostalgia. This is *it*. This is the day that God has given me. Let me live in it fully and purposefully." My mother, Jean McCarty, used to admonish me, "Today is a gift, tomorrow is only a promise. You don't know how long God has given you." She explained to me, many times, that none of us knows how long we've got to live. "Accidents happen, no matter how well one plans. You can be driving carefully in a well-maintained car and some maniac on drugs zooms through an intersection against the light and smashes into your car, ending your life. You just don't know how long you have." She went on to explain that we therefore must do our very best every day. You don't know if you'll ever see this person again, so say the good stuff that is in your heart for this person. If you appreciate or love or admire or respect them, tell them so right now. Her lessons caused me to be open to seeing many examples of wasted moments and missed opportunities. For example, Rick Ware, one of my graduate students, was the absolute best fifth- and sixth-grade teacher I ever met. He had a magic that could charm even the most disruptive, upset, behavior-disordered child. Yet he died of a very serious illness, prematurely, at the age of 38. We all behave as though we have all the time in the world. Did he have the chance to sing his song, dance his dance, say all those things he most wanted to say? Actually, in his case, I believe he did. He was a spectacularly open and loving teacher and managed to accomplish more in his short lifetime than many who taught until retirement age. Yet his death caused me to become clearer about my own work and my own desire to be more authentic, committed, and intentional about my mission in the world. That's what *"This is it"* means to me. Get out there and do it today. Do your very best. Give your all. As silly as it sounds, I sometimes hum the tune from the U.S. Army commercial, "Be all that you can be . . . " as I think about my day. Center yourself. Do it any way that works for you, but it is essential to remind yourself what you are about as part of your preparation process. Otherwise, your presentation can end up as an exercise in technique and slickness, style without substance. Do that enough, and you're ready for politics!

Self-Talk

Another way to think about this is to call it "self-talk." What sorts of things do you tell yourself as you get ready to do your work? "Oh, boy, this is a tough group today. They probably won't like what I have to say." Or, "This is going to be a great day. I have the unique opportunity to make a difference for 1,500 people today. I'm going to give them one heck of a great experience!" If you ever participated in sports on any level, did you have a coach who helped you do your best? Did your coach give a half-time talk that went, "We'll never make it. The team we're playing is so good that we are going to be eaten alive?" Never. Such a coach would be drummed out of the league for disabling his or her players. No, your coach told you that, despite the odds, you had a great chance of winning. He or she gave you a stack of reasons why you could really do this thing today. And that talk made a difference, very often. Well, you have to be your own coach today. What you say to yourself will affect your attitude. Your attitude, positive or negative, will affect your perceptions. You will see opportunities or you will be overwhelmed by obstacles, depending on your perceptions. And those perceptions will be acted upon. You will leap to take advantage of the situation if you see it as an opportunity or become defensive with low-energy if you see it as an obstacle. Self-talk is a crucial tool in your preparation process.

Distractions during the Day

You will have many distractions coming at you on the day of the presentation. These can include (but not be limited to):

1. *Difficulties with the room setup.* Get there early enough to obviate this problem. Send your room setup sheet, several times, to anyone involved. To the banquet staff if it's a hotel, to the meeting planner, to the committee or the person designated as in charge of audio-visual or room setup. Take a sneak peek at the room the night before, if possible. Weeks before the presentation, I usually ask my meeting planner to arrange this. I find that even if the room is set up perfectly, just seeing it in advance allows

me to visualize it and myself in it and a successful presentation taking place.

2. *Unhelpful people.* These can include the banquet setup crew, inexperienced conference committee members, or even your meeting planner, as well as early birds—participants who come too early and just have to talk to you while you're trying to get your materials and/or equipment (if any) set up. Sidestep the negative energy you encounter. Remind yourself that angry people are simply scared, confused, feeling inadequate, or ashamed. Empathize with them (for a brief moment), and then go on. Repeat your request quietly, calmly. Ask for what you want or need in a reasonable tone. If they can't or won't help, seek someone else. Ask your meeting planner to run interference for you. Don't put your energy into conflict today.

3. *Noise.* There may be blaring background music, loud groups, waiters shouting to each other as they set the tables, and so on. Ask to reduce the noise. Turn off the Muzak or supply your own tape with upbeat, positive music and ask for it to be played. I bring my own tape recorder and an album of cassettes I've prepared with music chosen for specific impacts I want to achieve. I plug it in to the PA system and control that variable.

4. *Emotional push from your contact person, the committee, or others.* "My career is riding on your presentation. Don't let me down!" Reassure these people. "I am going to do my very best. I have prepared a great presentation for you." If you don't believe in yourself, they cannot. You've got to project your belief. This, although it can be a distraction, is actually the beginning of your motivational talk—you are motivating your committee or contact and keeping them on track.

5. *A long, boring, or irrelevant speaker preceding you.* "And that brings us to page 26 of the new state regulations for health and safety." If you know in advance that the preceding event or speaker may be an energy drain for the group, ask your meeting planner if there can be a small stretch break just before you go on. If not, use a funny,

high-energy opening. Or ask the audience to rise and stretch. Do one of the energizing strategies I discuss in Chapter 3, "What Motivates People?" Ask people to find a partner sitting near themselves and ask that partner two or three questions that you provide. Sample questions for interaction in pairs might include:

a. How difficult or easy was it for you to get to the meeting today?

b. What did you have for breakfast today, what were the other choices you could have had, and are you proud of the choice you made?

c. If I met someone who knew you when you were 16, how would he or she describe you? In what ways are you different today?

d. If you won the lottery for $50 million, what's the first five things you'd spend money on?

e. Tell me something funny that's happened to you in the past three months.

f. Tell me three things that you're looking forward to in the next three months.

g. If you had a magic wand and could change this company (or school or group) in three ways, what would they be?

h. What's the furthest away you've ever been from the place you were born?

i. Tell me three things you've done in your job that you're most proud of.

j. How similar or different is the job you have today from what you wanted to do when you were in high school?

k. What was your nickname when you were a kid? How did you get it?

l. What is a skill you have that most people wouldn't guess?

m. If you could live anywhere in the world, where would you choose?

n. Name three people, not including your parents, from whom you've learned the most.

o. If you overheard other employees grumbling in the lunchroom, what could be their topic?

Give them three minutes to get engaged in the talk, and then sound your gong or bell or other musical signal for quiet. By getting them interacting, you've wakened them, as well as raising their positive expectation. (Any set of questions easy to answer can do. You could get them involved in your topic by focusing the questions on that.)

6. *An uncomfortable room.* It may be too hot or cold, too drafty, ugly, with old and torn seating, smoky, or the like. Work these issues in advance whenever possible. However, if you arrive and the room is a big distraction, ask your meeting planner for help adjusting temperature, or whatever. In the worst case, you simply accept it and go on. Here's where your own mental discipline comes to the rescue. You do a little self-talk, "This room is basically unimportant to me. It's the group, our meeting, my message, that's important." In the words of the Rev. Jesse Jackson, you "keep your eyes on the prize." I have a poster in my office that says, "Bloom Where You're Planted." I visualize that and go on.

7. *An incompetent introducer whose introduction actually steals energy from the group.* It's a very good idea to contact your introducer in advance of the presentation day. Send a written introduction to the introducer thanking him or her for being your introducer, explaining that you will be depending on him or her to help you make the audience ready to hear your presentation. You can control this variable by writing it yourself. Print it out in readable phrases, not in sentences. Talk with him or her about the introduction and see if he or she wants to use yours or write one. Give permission to do so—as long as the following items (you decide on your minimums) are included. In your conversations, try to scope out whether the person is experienced or a novice. If experienced, trust him or her.

If a novice, offer suggestions such as: "Please try to get the group's complete attention before beginning the introduction. If you begin while folks are still talking or loudly eating and clinking glasses together, the group will not pay much attention to the intro, and it will be much harder for me to start. Please give the final line a big emphasis, *"Please join me in welcoming* _____ *!"* A novice introducer is usually very grateful for all the help he or she can get. See Figure 5.1, which is a sample of advice to send introducers.

8. *The meal.* Breakfast, lunch, or dinner can be lovely, but don't put your energy into it. Use your time to become fully present in the room. Talk with people at your table, or make the rounds of the room and the group and introduce yourself to participants. Become aware of them, their energy, their concerns. Listen to the buzz in the room—what are they excited about? It's a clue to how to reach them.

9. *A saboteur.* Yes, meetings do have these people. I call them "disappointed office-seekers" because every assassinated U.S. President was killed by someone who was unhappy at not getting something he wanted from the government. People who were "ordered to report" to the conference will tend to be negative, sarcastic, hoping to help prove it was a failure. I've had such people come up to me, a stranger, and say, "Will you please make your speech short? I want to get out of here," or some such negative comment. They aren't doing this by accident. Some part of them knows full well that they are hoping to steal your energy, undercut the effectiveness of the meeting, or otherwise throw a wrench into the machinery. Remind yourself (ah, that wonderful self-talk!) that this is an unhappy, frightened, confused person who feels incompetent, powerless, or ashamed and doesn't really know how to cope. Respond positively, "Thanks for reminding me! I hope to make this not only painless but, if you can believe it, even interesting and fun!" They may respond with more negativity, but your relentless positivism will either convert them (unlikely) or drive

Figure 5.1

Advice for Introducers

Hi, thank you for being my introducer. I will be depending on you to help make the audience ready to hear my presentation. Because I've been a presenter for many years, I've learned what "works" and what doesn't and I would like to help you by sharing some tips and tricks.

Most of the time, my introducer is a seasoned professional in his or her own field, but usually doesn't have a lot of experience introducing speakers. If you are an experienced introducer, please disregard this advice.

We share a goal: to help make this meeting the best, most memorable, and the most effective ever!

1. **Group business.** Get all the business done well before or after the speaker. Doing too much business can help the audience lose energy and attentiveness. It helps to have someone other than the introducer conduct the business so that the introducer is seen as giving "something new" and will therefore get more attention from the audience. Room changes, canceled sessions, bathroom locations, timing of the breaks, and so on, are legitimate business but should be done in such a way as not to lose the audience's interest.

2. **Getting the audience's attention.** Use the following strategies *before* you begin the introduction:

   a. **Musical signal.** I can provide you with a melodious musical gong that will definitely get the group's attention if you sound it *loudly* several times. You can provide your own or simply use the old "spoon hitting the water glass" method. The keys are *loudly* and *repeatedly.*

   b. **Ask for attention.** Don't forget to ask the group for their attention as you are using the musical signal. "I'd like everyone's full attention as our program is about to begin." Or, "Thank you for your attention. It's time to call our meeting to order and begin with our keynote speaker."

   c. **The silent pause.** *This is absolutely the most important secret for getting a group's attention.* Never try to shout over a group. Never try to begin the introduction while folks are still talking. This will signal the group that you don't mind if they talk throughout the entire presentation! After you've rung the signal and verbally asked for attention, simply get silent while looking attentively out at the group. Your silence and expectant look will really signal the group that it's time to get down to serious business.

   d. **Begin only when there is silence.** Only after the silent pause and after the group actually does quiet down totally, should you begin your introduction of the speaker.

   e. **Show no anger.** If the group is high energy, feisty, humorous, bantering with you or others, simply wait good-naturedly. No group likes to be "disciplined" or made to feel guilty. Smile, show patience, ask for their attention again. Never be exasperated.

Advice to Introducers (continued)

3. **High energy.** The group will, at least at the beginning of the speakers' presentation, reflect your energy and excitement. If you seem bored, listless, uninvolved, or uncaring, the group will get the signal that the presentation and the presenter are of little value. Show your own commitment and interest by your high energy.

4. **Your presenter's key information.** Why did you choose this speaker? Put that in your presentation. Also ask your speaker what he or she would like the audience to know. Include that. Keep the presentation short, short, short. The presenter's seven-page résumé will not impress the audience—it will in fact turn them off.

5. **Use phrasing.** Don't read long sentences in a monotone. Go through your introduction and mark (in pencil or highlighter) the "readable phrases" that will make sense to your audience.

6. **Vary your voice.** Change your volume and the inflection of your voice from phrase to phrase in order to keep their interest.

7. **Be personal.** If there is some personal experience you've had with this presenter or with his or her topic, let your audience know. It will help stimulate their interest.

8. **Get the names right.** Check with your presenter to get the correct pronunciation of his or her name.

9. **Practice several times.** This will help you immeasurably to avoid tripping over unfamiliar phrases, etc.

10. **Greet your presenter** as he or she comes to the podium or microphone, shake his or her hand and then leave the podium and return quickly to your seat.

OK, you've done it! Congratulations! I hope these suggestions help. Introducing someone is a key part of the success of the day, and your energy and commitment will make a big difference.

them away (likely). Just don't get hooked into an
extended dialogue. Thank them again, and move on to
another person.

Gather Your Intention

Just before your presentation, as you see the meeting begin or
the program coming close to the moment of your introduction, gather your intention. This is your moment of intense
self-talk: Remind yourself of your higher purpose, remind
yourself of this opportunity to help these people believe in
themselves fully again, that you have the chance to empower
this group to use their skills and talents for the greater good.

DO, GET, BE

One of my most important mentors has been Dr. Merrill
Harmin, Professor Emeritus at Southern Illinois University. A
great presenter to teacher and parent groups around the
country for many years, he has a disarmingly simple
approach to helping someone gather his or her intention and
do his or her very best work. He calls this "Do, Get, Be."

Merrill tells us that most people think almost exclusively
about what they are going to do. When thinking about an
upcoming holiday, for example, like Thanksgiving, your
friends or coworkers may ask, "What are you going to do for
Thanksgiving?" And we respond with the usual litany of
activities such as, "Visit my folks," or "Roast a big turkey and
have everyone over." So many holidays that we fantasize will
be delightful actually become sources of great stress and hurt
feelings. On the way to creating that holiday dinner, you find
yourself rushing around to get the house cleaned, the shop-
ping done, the cooking started. In the process, you may be
curt or even loudly angry at your children for making a mess

or being too noisy. You may have a fight with a spouse or an angry or depressing encounter with a family member who, anticipating rejection or nursing an old hurt, is already anxious and defensive about attending. And so it goes. (The highest suicide rate each year occurs around Thanksgiving, Christmas, and New Year's Day.)

Dr. Harmin reminds us that there may be two much more important questions to consider instead of "What are you going to *do*?" He reminds us to ask, "What would you like to *get* from this holiday?" When we ask that, we begin considering goals and intentions. Answering that question honestly about Thanksgiving, most people would say, "I want to get closer with my family. I'd like to become more aware of my gratitude to God for all the good that is in my life. I'd like to get a feeling of peace and contentment." Very few would say that they'd like to be angrier, or have a fight, or put on weight from overeating!

After answering that question, Dr. Harmin tells us to ask ourselves, "How do I have to *be* in order to get what I want?" And this question reminds us that what happens to us is not an accident. We have a big role in selecting outcomes for events by choosing our behavior, our attitudes, our responses. If I want peace, I probably have to be peaceful. If I want closeness, I probably have to show patience, love, and caring to my family. If I want to experience thanksgiving, I must express my thankfulness and become more aware of the spiritual dimensions of my life.

Do-Get-Be can play a big role in preparing oneself for a motivational speech. Ask yourself those three questions now about the speech you are planning to present. What am I going to do? Give a motivational speech to a group of employees of my company. What do I want to get out of this? I'd like to help them rediscover the fire they all had when the company was a shaky startup only 10 years ago. There was a magic spirit in the company I hope to help them all recover. How do I have to be? Here's the most important question. Perhaps I have to be focused on my own fire, my own commitment? Perhaps I need to listen to other employees' feelings about the company and their hopes and dreams, too? You see? Do-Get-Be can be a powerful mental focusing tool to remind us of the most important parts of motivational speaking.

DEALING WITH YOUR FEAR AND ANXIETY

It isn't easy to get up in front of a group, under even the most ideal circumstances. Public speaking challenges our self-concept (who we think we are), our self-image (how we think we look or come across to others), and our self-esteem (how worthwhile we think we are.) Facing a speech, we can experience considerable anxiety that can rob us of our energy and distract us from remembering our message. You can cope with this anxiety with some fairly simple strategies.

1. *Be fully prepared.* As long as you've done your homework, you can at least have confidence in your preparation.
2. *Imagine or visualize success.* Think about succeeding. Imagine what it will look like when you are confidently and competently speaking to an appreciative audience. (Don't self-sabotage by imagining a hostile group!)
3. *Change the physical cues that escalate anxiety.* When we are anxious, some physical symptoms can occur that we have learned to associate with stress, fear, or anxiety, such as rapid, shallow breathing, rapid heart rate, high distractibility, coldness and clamminess in hands and feet, flushed feeling in the face and neck, nausea, teeth clenching or grinding. As we become aware of such symptoms, our very awareness of them causes us to feel even more anxious. This can become self-reinforcing.

    To reverse this effect, work at reversing the symptom. For example, go into the bathroom and run a sink of really hot water—as hot as you can stand to put your hands in safely. Soak your hands in the hot water for about five minutes. As your hands warm, you will very probably find yourself calming and your heart rate slowing. You are simulating calm with warm hands and fooling your body into believing that you are feeling calmer. It usually works!

Try breathing slowly and regularly. Find a quiet place to sit without distractions. Often, the meeting will have a "green room" or ready room for presenters. That can be a good place. Sit there, close your eyes, and begin counting your breaths. Don't try to make them faster or slower; don't try to make them deeper or shallower. Just count your breaths. Each inhalation counts for one and each exhalation counts for another. Keep your eyes closed, and simply count your breaths. When you get to 50 or so, you will probably find that you are feeling quite calm and relaxed—again, by simulating the breathing pattern of a calm person.

4. *Become aware of your positive feelings for your audience.* Quietly and with feeling, send them your blessing. Express, perhaps in the form of a prayer, your hopes and wishes for their success and your gratitude for being allowed to do this piece of work with them. Bless the family that you came from for helping you, guiding you, and preparing you for this day. This brings you back to that still, small voice in the core of you that we call values, or spirituality, or soul. It is such a major source of our power and the goodness in our lives. Acknowledge it. Use the forms of whatever religious tradition you come from or invent your own.

5. *Arrive early.* Arriving late creates a rushed, off-center, apologetic, out-of-touch feeling. We cannot connect as well with our audience when we are feeling that way. To the extent physically possible, arrive early. If you do find yourself coming off a delayed flight and being rushed to the convention center, racing down hallways with minutes to spare, it's time to take two extra minutes to calm yourself and five minutes to slow your breathing down and even a few minutes to set out your slides. Although

you are delayed, the audience knows the problem and sympathizes with you. When you begin, acknowledge the lateness, and your being out of breath, tell a quick lateness story if you have one, and then get into the talk.

6. *Embrace the fear.* Examine where it's coming from. Is it from your desire to perform well? Isn't that desire a good one? Is it from a lack of confidence? Doesn't that fear motivate you to do more preparation and become more competent? Odd as it may sound, fear has an important role to play in our personal growth. When I have fear, it's an important marker announcing to me the next areas in which I have to do my growing, learning, and changing. When I get too comfortable, I know that it is time to risk something. A new topic, a new kind of group to work with, a new style of presenting, or a new strategy. I've learned that fear can be my teacher. I am not delighted with fear, but I don't have to fear the fear!

7. *Face the sources of fear in the audience.* Sometimes the fear is based, for me, in the audience. There's someone there, a constituency, with whom I've had trouble connecting. Or I've been told, "Those physical education teachers are not going to be happy campers at the meeting today." A strategy that has proved its value for me is to go directly to those people in the audience whom I most fear and shake their hands. I've learned that the resisters in an audience sit in fairly well-defined areas—the last two or three rows, of course; the seats nearest to the exits, wherever they are; along the outside aisles on both sides from about the middle of the room to the back; the aisle seats in the center aisle(s) in the back third of the room. Very rarely do I find resisters sitting in the front five rows. I make it my practice, almost always, if there is enough time, to go to these areas and make eye contact with individuals. I then extend my hand and shake theirs while introducing myself. "Hi, I'm Hanoch McCarty. I'm your speaker this morning. I'm glad to meet you. What do you do for this company?" Occasionally I'm given a snide answer like, "I wait for retirement." Mostly, however, people are charmed by this greeting. "You're the first keynote speaker who

ever came over to talk to me," is the typical response. I go on to promise, "You know, I've been a member of the audience at a lot of conferences and workshops, so I know enough to value your time, and I am going to work as hard as I possibly can to make this a worthwhile day for you!" It's amazing how disarming it is, to promise an individual to do my very best for him or her personally. Also amazing to me is this secret that I've discovered—it's much easier for people to be rude to a total stranger. Once I've introduced myself, the people who had planned to read the newspaper during my talk are much less willing to do that. We've got a relationship, after all. I find out what they do and try to quickly relate to it in some way. "Oh, you teach English? I taught English for seven years at the high school level, too." "You're a personnel manager? Difficult work, isn't it? I am responsible for hiring, firing, interviewing, and training at my little company, and it's one of the toughest things I have to do. What's your secret in picking good people?" Asking someone's advice is also a very disarming strategy.

8. *Practice your talk enough to build confidence.* First run through it with a timer. See how it goes. Do it out loud so you can hear the tone of it. Then do it on tape. Then play back a short segment of the tape to check your delivery. You can practice it repeatedly with a tape recorder, always listening to one or two short segments to give yourself feedback. Graduate to a trial with a caring friend or trusted colleague. Do a small section of the talk, and ask your friend for impressions, not a full critique. Ask your friend to complete this sentence: "When I heard that, I felt . . . " Practice standing up just as you will deliver the speech. Try to replicate the actual speaking situation as much as you can.

9. *Take care of your voice.* In the days prior to a presentation, one can become tense without being very conscious of it. That, along with dehydration often associated with air travel, can cause one to develop a rough voice, hoarseness, or even laryngitis. Now you are really worried: How can you get up and do a speech without a voice? There

are some simple things you can do to help with this problem. The best treatment is to go into total vocal rest until you have to give your speech. No whispering, no talking whatever. Buy an over-the-counter throat pain spray. They are surprisingly good, as are products like Aspergum. Gargling with warm salt water helps as does hydrating yourself by drinking enough water every day. All singers and professional speakers know to avoid milk products when they are going to perform. They cause the production of mucus and roughen the voice. Avoid anything that might affect your voice—smoking or being around smokers, foods that tend to make you cough (if any), and yelling or straining your voice.

Once I was on a flight to Boston to give the opening keynote address at a huge national convention. I was beside myself because I had very bad laryngitis. I could barely make myself understood. How was I going to give my speech? I did not know. On the flight, my seatmate was a lady who looked like the stereotypical opera singer. She had a beautiful voice and started or attempted to start a conversation with me. I made signs and a few whispers in return. She asked, "What do you do?" I signed and whispered, *"I'm a professional speaker!"* She laughed, "I'll bet you're on your way to give an important speech!" I nodded. "How would you like to get your voice back?" I nodded frantically. She then proceeded to tell me her secret formula. "Take a cup of steaming hot water, hot enough to make a cup of tea; but don't use any tea. Add to it several teaspoons of honey and a generous amount of lemon juice. Then add two shakes of cayenne pepper." I looked surprised. After all, I had been given tea and honey with lemon by my mother when I had a throat cold but had never heard of putting cayenne pepper in the mix. She smiled, "Look, the honey and the lemon don't really do much for your throat. Much of the help you get from this is from the hot water. Don't use cold drinks when you are speaking or singing. Hot water opens up the passages. But the big secret is the cayenne pepper. It contains a drug called *capsaicin,* which is a powerful anti-inflammatory. You can get it in a prescription form for a lot more money and trouble or simply use two shakes of cayenne pepper. Mix it all together, and force yourself to drink it. Truly, the cayenne pepper makes it tough to drink, but that's why you have the honey and the lemon—to kill the taste of the pepper! Drink it all down. And wait about 30 minutes and you'll have your voice back—or most of it—for about an hour or so." When I looked skeptical, she said, "I'm an opera singer. I don't get paid unless I sing. This secret has saved me many times. But don't abuse your voice, and do go back into total vocal rest right after your speech. This drink doesn't cure anything, it simply reduces the swelling in your vocal folds long enough for you to give your presentation." I wish I had taken that woman's name and address so I could thank her profusely for this information. It worked! And it's worked many times since. I would caution you that this advice came from an opera singer, not a physician. So, as a palliative for occasional use, it is all right; however, if you are experiencing hoarseness or throat problems regularly, see your doctor immediately.

10. *Consider getting voice coaching.* A good voice coach can help you learn to use your vocal instrument more effectively and produce your voice in ways that will help you avoid or at least diminish the number of times you experience hoarseness or laryngitis. Your voice, after coaching, will most likely sound much more pleasant and mellifluous, and you will project it more effectively.

Remember that you are here to motivate the audience. With that end in mind, these tips and tricks may help you cope with the often inevitable stress and anxiety of public speaking so that your own infectious motivation and commitment can show.

6 OWNING THE SPACE

Many speakers arrive, enter the room, sit where they are told, get up, give their talk, and leave. They accept the room as it is. They take the setup as a given. Indeed, there are many times when it is impossible to do otherwise. The room has been set up for the conference's other speakers, other events, and other goals. However, when possible, it is very useful for the motivational speaker to take steps to own the environment, to place a personal stamp on the space.

THE CORPORATE SALES MEETING

The audience entered the room, not as a group but as many groups, twos and threes, individuals and quartets. About 40 minutes prior to the meeting, the first two people arrived, selected widely separated seats and then went outside looking for coffee.

The room was a typical meeting room in a downtown hotel. The walls had a nondescript wallpaper in dark shades of mauve almost matching the colors in the floral carpeting. Up front at the left was a table and an overhead projector, and a rather small projection screen was set up behind it. In the center, on a short riser facing the aisle, was a podium with the hotel chain's logo emblazoned near the top. A microphone on a gooseneck showed above the rim of the podium.

Bland music, often called "elevator music," played in the background, ignored by all.

The lighting was dimmed somewhat, lending a dingy quality to the room. Only one spotlight shone on the podium.

Chairs, some new, some rather battered, stood in straight rows on either side of a wide main aisle. Although the meeting was to be attended by only about 300 people, more than 400 chairs were set out. At the back wall, a table was set with hundreds of glasses and about 20 pitchers of ice water. To its right was another, larger table, with coffee, tea, fruit juice, and donuts. Small gluey Danish pastries sat heaped in a circular arrangement at the back of the table.

A small gray banner, about two feet high and six feet long, duct-taped to the wall behind the podium, proclaimed the name and logo of this small but growing national company.

Outside the room by the door sat two women, secretaries to the conference planner, with registration materials and packets of information for the participants. Each wore a "Welcome" badge and smiled as each participant registered. The keynote speaker stood, back to the group that was entering, and adjusted slides and materials on the table next to the projector. Then the speaker went to the riser and sat on one of the three chairs next to the podium and waited expectantly, occasionally reviewing notes. Although she always provided handout materials when conducting a seminar, this was a motivational speech, and she had not given the conference planner any handouts for the participants' packets.

The participants, mostly seated by now, balanced coffee cups and pastries on their laps, talked loudly with old friends and colleagues, thumbed through the conference packets; a few still wandered about.

The conference planner strode to the podium along with the company sales manager, who sat beside the speaker and briefly said hello. The conference planner tapped the microphone. "Good morning, ladies and gentlemen, it's time to begin CarrTech's Third National Sales Meeting!" The noise in the room only abated a little. "Really! It's time to begin! You'll have a chance to network a bit later. Good morning!" About half the group responded, "Good Morning!" The rest of the audience quieted at that, although quite a few side conversations persisted for the next five or six minutes through the introductions. The meeting began.

A DIFFERENT, MORE EFFECTIVE, CORPORATE SALES MEETING

The audience entered the room, not as a group but as many groups, twos and threes, individuals and quartets. About 40 minutes prior to the meeting, the first two people arrived, selected widely separated seats and then went outside looking for coffee.

The room was a typical meeting room in a downtown hotel. The walls had a nondescript wallpaper in dark shades of mauve almost matching the colors in the floral carpeting. Up front at the center was a table and an overhead projector, and large projection screen was set up in the corner. To the right of the table and projector, on a short riser, was a podium A microphone on a gooseneck showed above the rim of the podium. The speaker had covered the hotel's logo on the podium with a two-foot-wide colorful paper sign she had prepared with the theme of the conference, "Sales through Spectacular Service!"

Chairs were set in straight rows—the left and right sides angled to face the screen.

Bright, energetic music (a cassette provided by the speaker), played softly over the PA system, its upbeat rhythms contributing to a feeling of energy and expectation.

Outside the room by the door sat two women, secretaries to the conference planner, with registration materials and packets of information for the participants. Each wore a "Welcome" badge and smiled as each participant registered.

The speaker had provided camera-ready copy for handouts reinforcing her themes and concepts and had asked for them to be duplicated on colored paper.

On every chair was a sheet, provided by the speaker, with inspirational quotations, some from famous authors, some from members of the company sales team—quotes she had obtained through telephone interviews.

On all the walls of the room were a dozen bright posters, prepared by the speaker, each focusing on one major concept she planned to cover. The speaker had help from the corporate advertising office, which did the final artwork on the posters from the designs she had provided. "You can use these later throughout the company," she told them.

The participants, encouraged to their seats by ushers (a suggestion the speaker had made to the conference planner), balanced coffee cups and pastries on laps, talked with old friends and colleagues, thumbed through the conference packets. Many were reading the speaker's handout material.

The conference planner strode to the podium along with the company sales manager and the speaker, who had made sure to contact, meet, and speak with the sales manager prior to the conference and again that morning. The conference planner tapped a small gong (provided by the speaker), which emitted a loud musical note grabbing everyone's attention. "Good morning, ladies and gentlemen, it's time to begin CarrTech's Third National Sales Meeting! And have we got a treat for you this morning!"

The common wisdom about business success usually is given as "to succeed in business everything is location, location, location." Or it may be given to you as "timing, timing, timing." In this case, the advice to a motivational speaker would be: *environment, environment, environment!* I watched a brilliant and dramatic keynote speaker be half as effective as I had seen him be many times before because he was stuck up on a dais, behind a podium, with a fixed microphone and flanked on either side by people staring at the audience from the head. Known for his almost evangelical style, he was hemmed in, his usual fiery and high-energy delivery muted and lacking in spirit. Halfway through, he clearly couldn't take it any more. He strode off the dais, stepped in front of it, grabbed the microphone from its clip on the podium, and continued his talk standing on the same level as the audience. With freedom to move (he yanked a length of cable from under the dais), he moved among the tables. His gestures increased in frequency and intensity. The audience was transfixed. He had rescued a potential failure by taking over the environment.

Conferences of large diverse groups can be different from intact groups who work together regularly. Intact groups can have an insularity that can sometimes defend them against hearing the speaker's ideas fully and fairly. When the group enters their own meeting room, on their own territory, you can be seen as the interloper. The inside jokes and comments and their familiarity with the environment can work together to make it much harder for you, the speaker, to reach your audience. By owning the environment, you change things enough that the audience, upon entering, feels unconsciously that they have entered *your* space, not theirs. It disarms them and makes them much more receptive to you.

WAYS OF OWNING THE ENVIRONMENT

There are many techniques for making sure that the room works with you rather than against you. First, you must begin by scouting the space. If you are a thousand miles away, this can be done by speaking to your meeting planner at some length about the room and its setup. You can call the banquet staff if it is to be at a hotel or by finding the person(s) responsible for that space no matter where it might be—an auditorium, convention center, a public space, or whatever. Many such places have room diagrams to help conventions plan. If you can go to the space days prior to the event, it is a plus. Certainly, arriving well in advance of the meeting is the minimum preparation. See how the room is being prepared. If you send out a room setup sheet or packet, you will find that many venues will have their own habits and preferences and a very busy and often overworked setup crew. They have many other things on their minds, like the setting up of six other rooms that have to be done right away. You may be seen as a minor annoyance in their day. Your concerns may not be theirs, so your being there to make sure things are done correctly can be essential.

YOUR EXPERTISE EXTENDS
BEYOND THE SUBJECT MATTER

You may think that you've been hired, engaged, or asked to speak simply because of your particular knowledge or skill as a speaker on this subject. However, your meeting planner may have an unconscious expectation that you will tell him or her how to organize at least your part of the meeting for success. Remember that your host may be an expert in his or her own field but is not usually an expert in speaking or conference planning. Any suggestions that you can give will usually be appreciated. The best meeting planners are easy to work with, experienced, and thoughtful about both the audience's and the speaker's needs and concerns. Some very few meeting planners take a know-it-all stance, and it's best to avoid confrontations with such people. Play it their way to the extent that you can, because it is their group, after all. Your goal is to leave them looking good for having chosen you, isn't it?

OWN THE SPACE PHYSICALLY!

If the meeting planner is open to suggestions about the environment (you find out by asking!), provide your suggestions,

and make it clear that they are not demands, only suggestions. Work with this person to help create the best environment for you and for all the presenters who precede or follow
you. Brainstorm with your host any ideas that will enhance
the environment. Doing so will be appreciated because (1) it
makes the meeting planner a full participant in the process;
(2) it's a learning experience for both of you; and (3) you will
definitely come up with better and more focused ideas than if
you tried it alone. It can be a very good idea to prepare your
suggestions as a checklist that you can send to all the meeting planners with whom you work.

To Dais or Not to Dais

There is no one correct answer as to whether or not the
speaker should be up on a dais or riser. Certainly, if you are
speaking to a large group (any group over 400), it will help
those at the back to see you if you are on a riser. Speakers
who are action oriented will find themselves moving off the
dais and back on at various moments in their presentations.
Tony Robbins is often seen with a thrust stage setup in which
a wide riser has a peninsula jutting far out into the audience,
almost like a fashion-show runway. Carrying a wireless microphone, he moves out into the audience on this thrust stage
(his groups are huge!) and back again. This arrangement gives
him lots of visibility while also affording him the opportunity
to move about maintaining visual interest. He has strategi-
cally placed chairs, stools, and tables that allow him to sit, to
stand and move, to seem casual by sitting on the edge of a
table, and so on. And talk about controlling a room—he is
the absolute master! His team of associates have scouted the
room, working assiduously with the convention center staff,
and they've brought in their own sound equipment, lighting,
and other support services. Video walls, projection TV

screens, elaborate technology have been chosen by his team, never left to chance. You may not have access to those resources, but his example of attention to detail is worth emulating.

Some speakers are more formal and want a dais and podium, or at least a podium, no matter the size of the group. What's important is: Make your needs known, and make sure that your requests are followed, whenever possible. If there is some reason that your requests cannot be accommodated, at least know that in advance so that you can plan around it and get yourself mentally prepared for it. Being surprised by an inappropriate or incorrect setup can be disorienting and steal your energy, distract your thinking, and move your mood from the upbeat and optimistic mood necessary for the motivational speaker to a mood of anger, upset, or resentment, which will undermine your ability to do the job.

Lights! Action! Camera! Music!

Most meeting rooms begin as relatively neutral spaces. The standard décor of meeting rooms or ballrooms will be ignored by the audience unless it is quite unusual: The spectacular ballroom of a brand-new, first-class hotel, for example, will draw comments from the crowd. A bare space with faded and peeling paint, dirty and ripped carpeting, or other disastrous problems will also draw commentary from those attending. Beginning with that neutral décor, in hotels and convention centers, the banquet staff will skirt the tables, put out the usual flowers, plants, or other items the conference has requested. You, the speaker, can add your own ownership décor that can powerfully support your message. Posters with slogans, logos, new products, and new programs will focus the group on the day's purpose. Colorful banners with the key phrase you will use, or that extol the virtues of the company, program, product line, group, or philosophy that will be your major focus can really help your effectiveness.

Using posters and banners may seem to be a cliché, but they actually do add a lot in helping to create a space that actively supports your message. This is not the Bijou Hotel's ballroom anymore, it is *your* space, *your* program's milieu. Participants entering the room, expecting the normal meeting space, are immediately immersed in the environmental cues you've arranged. That makes them much more receptive to your spoken message. The ideas here may or may not be within your scope as the speaker. Some may be too expensive, elaborate, or impractical for you, the speaker, to provide, especially if you are traveling some distance and are not part of the company or group to whom you'll be speaking. However, if you can utilize any of these suggestions, the effect will be dramatic and powerful. If you can suggest any of these to your meeting planner and engage the company's help and resources in this effort, your impact will be increased considerably.

Decorate with Light

If you are the very first presenter (after the introduction), make sure your exciting, well-designed, and colorful title slide is up on the screen. This establishes who is speaking and what your topic will be and reassures the audience that they have come to the correct room. If you are going to be on after several other presenters, this will usually not be possible. I usually do a service for my clients of creating an exciting title slide with the logo of their organization, the title of the conference or its theme, and the date and place. I put that up on the screen so that the room becomes clearly one supporting that conference and group. I have been complimented and thanked more times than I can count by grateful meeting planners for this little gesture.

If you want a spotlight on you, it is necessary to ask for that well before the meeting date. Many hotel meeting rooms have spotlights, but these may not be aimed where you want them, and there are often union rules about who can move them and when. These things are not easy to get at the last minute. How bright do you want the lights in the room to be? Do you want them dimmed? If you tend to stay up front or on stage or at the podium during your talk, keeping the lights dimmed except for spots up front will work well. If you like to repeatedly enter the audience, having all the lights up bright will probably be best. I find that having lights go up suddenly and dim down throughout the talk is a distraction that steals attention, unless you have a good assistant who knows how to dim slowly and in concert with your cues. I've seen an excellent speaker who provided colored gels for spotlights and who used color to cue the audience—when speaking about the company's early red-ink era, the lights slowly dimmed until only the red-gelled lights were on (except for the speaker's spotlight). When the current, high profit era was mentioned, the lights turned green. Every time "business as usual" was mentioned, the red lights would be brought up; and when the high-energy, total-commitment style of doing business was mentioned, the green lights gradually became brighter. This brought laughter and dramatically drove home the point.

Decorate with Color

These suggestions are among those I may share with the meeting planner since most are usually beyond the scope of the out-of-town speaker flying in to give a talk. Change the lighting to colored bulbs, put up panels of brightly colored cloth, add displays of flowers. Anything that makes the room seem festive will be a change from the normal work environment. People feel valued when the company or group has gone to some lengths to make the room beautiful. If it is a luncheon or dinner talk, ask if there will be floral center-pieces. They do add a lot—as long as they are not large enough to distract or interfere with conversation across the tables. Many meeting rooms in newer or refurbished hotels and conference centers have surfaces finished with a cloth that works with Velcro and facilitates the hanging of banners, posters, and other items without damage. I routinely put the hook type of Velcro stickers on the back of all my posters and banners. Traveling with banners can be difficult unless you visit an art supply store and purchase a sturdy artist's portfolio. These are available in a number of sizes, and one can easily be found that will fit the size of poster you have chosen. They have zippered edges and strong carrying handles and can be checked with the airlines. For those presentations where I like to use posters, I have made up a set of posters and store them in this case, ready to go on the next journey. For each presentation I usually prepare at least a couple of highly specific posters as part of my customization of each talk to fit the group. Remember that schools have school colors and many companies have their company colors and logos, which you can use on these posters to reinforce your customizing image.

In working with a school group, I often ask if some of the elementary school classes can be asked to help decorate the teacher's meeting. Their drawings, posters, and banners are a delight that the teachers and/or parents enjoy considerably.

With one corporate group, I conducted a written survey of employees on attitudes and their views of the company's needs and likelihood of success in the near term. Some of the answers I received were so articulate and perceptive, I contacted those employees and asked permission to quote them directly. Almost all agreed. Instead of simply verbally quoting them, I greatly enlarged the relevant sections of their questionnaires (Kinko's does a great job at this!) onto poster boards, which I put up on the walls around the room and out in the lobby around the coffee table. These positive quotes became the framework around which I built my speech. Those employees were delighted, as were their peers and their supervisors.

Decorate with Music

As my audience enters, there is music playing, music that I have chosen and supplied. The music is upbeat, energetic without being frantic, and it's on at a volume that doesn't overwhelm or call too much attention to itself. I am already affecting the mood and receptivity of my audience. Don't let the hotel or conference center play its usual bland "elevator music" in the background. Choose music that reinforces your message, subtly or not. High-energy music, music with an appropriate theme, music has a unique power to move the human spirit. Does the company, school, or group have a theme song, fight song, or alma mater? Don't be ashamed to play it. Can you think of any music that will connect to your speech's message? Use it! Play music at a volume that is just loud enough to perceive but not loud enough to distract or annoy. The piano music of Scott Joplin, baroque compositions, Mozart violin trios and quartets seem to please many people and keep the energy high. Avoid music with words unless the music is particularly appropriate to the meeting, the themes, or the group.

A note about controlling the music: I bring along an inexpensive cassette recorder and an adapter plug that will connect with the three-prong Canon or XLR connectors found on most PA systems. You can get these adapters at any Radio Shack or electronics store. This allows me to control the timing and volume and choice of selection before and during my talk. Larger venues such as major convention centers or conference halls will usually have a control booth and technician who will work with you and run the cassettes for you on your cue. Make sure you go over your cues with this technician carefully. I use music at a number of points in my presentations as well as some sound effects. It can be disastrous if your technician forgets a cue or is distracted at the key moment. If you are using a presentation program such as PowerPoint, you can print out a set of speaker's notes and put your cues on these, and your technician can more easily follow along and anticipate when tapes are to be played or other special effects cued up.

Decorate with Handouts

A mini-poster summarizing major points; a short, succinct article espousing your point of view; a sheet of pithy quotes along the same lines—any of these, placed on every participant's chair, will set them up to view your presentation more favorably by the time you begin. Print the handouts on colored paper stock. If there are several items, use different colors to make it easy to refer to a particular section. These will find their way back to offices or classrooms and will sell your ideas (and you) for years to come.

Many speakers have learned to have "pass-outs" or souvenir items that reinforce their message and also become a part of their marketing strategy. Putting your business card on every chair or at every place at each table is one example. I have a humorous item I designed more than 20 years ago called Narrow Pads®, which I put on every chair. It's a pad of paper only 1 inch wide but about $8^1/_2$ inches long that says "For taking notes when dealing with narrow minded people." These get a big response and give me an opening with the group as I begin speaking about being receptive to new ideas.

Such items create readiness to listen on the part of your audience. A great speaker of my acquaintance, Florence Littauer, author of *Silver Boxes: The Gift of Encouragement,** places silver box centerpieces and various other silver-themed items at every table and around the room. She has many items designed to play upon these themes that strongly support her presentation. She is the absolute master of coordinated themes in presentations.

Other speakers distribute what I call "value-added" items such as credit-card-sized laminated summary cards with all the key points included. Of course, on the back you will find information on how to contact that speaker.

Decorate with Furniture

Some room arrangements work against certain kinds of presentations. Ask for what you need, remembering of course that many times you'll have to accept the arrangement as a given because it has been set up for other parts of the conference. If you wish to do a presentation that has a considerable amount of audience interaction in small groups, seating in an auditorium will be less conducive to your plan than would seating in a flat-floored large room with movable chairs. I have found that the meeting room with those narrow tables at which participants sit with their writing materials is great for note-taking at a workshop or an informative speech but diminishes the energy at a motivational speech because it separates and distances the participants from each other and from the speaker.

Too Many Chairs, Not Enough People!

Beware the problem of a small number of people in a sea of chairs. If you are presenting in a room with movable chairs, there is a great tendency for the meeting planners to

---

*Littauer, Florence. *Silver Boxes: The Gift of Encouragement*. Dallas, TX: Word Publishing, 1989.

overestimate how many people will attend. Their hopes for a large group are translated into large numbers of chairs. The custodian or setup crew will also add to that because they don't like being called upon at the last minute to put out more chairs in a hurry. If the conference had 200 attendees last year, the meeting planner will estimate 300 for this year. The custodian, hearing 300, will put out at least 350 "for insurance." When 80 people show up, they are lost in that space. Ask your meeting planner what advance registration has indicated. Help him or her revise the estimate more realistically. Then have some rows (from the back) removed. If extra chairs are to be stored "just in case," have them placed out of the sight of the incoming audience. If those extra chairs are placed at the back of the room, the incoming audience will unstack them and set them up at the back because of their aversion to sitting down front.

Rows that are too far apart will do the same thing. Another example of an environmental setting that diminishes your effectiveness is the auditorium with way too many seats for the group attending. People will tend to sit in the back and the middle sections, with the first eight or ten rows almost completely empty. Clusters will seat themselves along the far back wall on both sides. There is a critical mass necessary for a group to catch the fire of your presentation. Even in a very large room, if you can bunch the people together, you can get this powerful group effect to work with you to reach the audience most effectively. Too much space between them will drain that energy away before the group effect can work at all. I send rolls of the very brightly colored tape that is used to cordon off construction areas (available at most hardware stores) to my meeting planner along with little printed cards that declare boldly, THESE ROWS ARE CLOSED and ask that the back rows be roped off when I know that I'll be speaking to 300 hundred people in a space with 2,000 chairs.

I also ask the committee to provide ushers because there are always individuals who will climb over the ropes or tapes or even pull them down in order to sit in the back rows. As soon as one sits there, lots of others will join him or her.

Send your meeting planner a *room setup plan* (see Figure 6.1 at the end of this chapter) with a list of your needs. Make sure that a copy is also sent to the banquet manager of the hotel or conference center, the custodian of the school, or whoever is in charge of the space you'll be speaking in. I've also discovered, over many years of public speaking, that these room setup plans have a way of disappearing, so I mail a second copy about a week or so prior to my speeches. Bring several with you. If you arrive early and find the room has not been set as you requested, don't complain, simply ask again for the setup to be done the way you need. Don't be afraid to pitch in and help move chairs and tables if that is what it takes. The example of you doing that work will often motivate others to pitch in, too.

Pay attention to the details that can either enhance or detract from your presentation. If you like to leave the stage, come in front of the podium, and enter the audience during your speech, you'll need a wireless microphone (or at least a mike with a long cord) and you may want the stairs (usually to the side of the riser) to be placed in front. Reduce the number of items that can stress you and distract from your focus.

Decorate with Hidden Surprises

Entering the room early, long before the first participant arrives, I've taped five envelopes under certain randomly selected chairs. Each envelope is numbered. In each sealed envelope, there is a question. As I begin my talk, I ask the audience to reach under their chairs and feel around for an envelope. They are found. "Don't open them," I ask, "until I call on you. Will the owner of envelope number one open it and ask me the question you find inside?" This person does so and my talk is under way as I answer that "question from the audience." Having answered it, I present the participant with a signed copy of *A 4th Course of Chicken Soup for the Soul* as a gift. The audience applauds as I then ask the possessor of envelope number two to ask that question. This can be a nice and effective audience involvement technique.

Sometimes I only put one item under a chair—such as a coupon announcing that this person is the winner of the door prize. And, speaking of door prizes, I've done the corny thing of having an old door gift wrapped with an enormous red ribbon and bow and, after choosing the door prize winner, having that door brought in as the prize. Corny as it may be, it's always been greeted with laughter and applause (as well as good-natured groans) as I then give the person his or her real gift.

Surprises can be built into the way you've set up the room, pleasant surprises that will entertain, amuse, and sustain the audience's attention and create positive feelings about your presentation.

Food and Water!

Most hotels and conference centers will provide a water station—a table with pitchers of ice-water and glasses—at the rear of the speaking room. This is very good. What I find disturbing is the setup of a coffee and tea station inside the speaking room. If possible, I request that coffee, tea, and snacks be set up outside the speaking room, because the constant stream of people going for refills, the clinking of cups and saucers, and the stirring of spoons is a real distraction, as is the smell of the coffee.

If, for some unforeseeable reason, you find yourself in a room that is drawing attention from the group, and there is no way to ameliorate the problems before the speech began, then neutralize the problem by acknowledging it. Comment on it, but be gentle. Don't criticize, because the owner of the room or the person who chose it—and his or her friends—may be an important part of your audience.

When you are preparing for your next motivational speech, think of the environment and everything you can do to own it. Never forget how powerfully the context affects the outcome. Just as water assumes the shape of its container, a speech can take on the qualities, for good or ill, of the space in which it is presented.

OWN THE SPACE PSYCHOLOGICALLY!

The audience is outside the room, in a large foyer, milling about in small groups and clusters, holding their coffee cups and donuts, chatting and reconnecting. It's been a long time for many of them since they've had the opportunity to see old friends and colleagues. You, the keynote speaker, have been here for a long time. Your presentation is set up, the electronics have been tested, the slides are in order, the room looks great. Where are you? You are out there, in the foyer, mingling with the crowd. You approach a small group and say, "Excuse me for interrupting. I am _____ and I am your keynote speaker this morning. I want to introduce myself and get to meet you personally before I meet you 'generically' in there (nodding toward the auditorium doors)." You read a name tag. "Johanna Smed. What do you do?" She tells you her job title. "How long have you been with the company?" She answers, smiling. You go on to the second and third people in the trio. "Great meeting you. I do hope you like my presentation. I'll be talking about the secrets of five-star service, and I hope to make it fascinating to you!" You leave the group and zip over to another. These are fast, almost lightning visits to a series of groups in the foyer. If you can do six or eight of them in a half-hour, you will have a huge impact on the entire group. The word gets around the group incredibly quickly. "That's the keynote speaker. He is introducing himself personally to people. I never saw any speaker do that before. Wow! I'll bet he's going to be great!"

After a few of these, you go on into the meeting room. You stop along the way and do the same thing with small trios and quartets of participants who are already seated. You thank them for coming. Perhaps you arrange for someone to "volunteer" at a key moment during your presentation. (I always promise an autographed copy of my latest book if they'll volunteer, and I never fail to get several willing participants.) During these little mini-interviews, I glean important information about their energy, mood, and feelings about the conference and the company or association or school they represent. I even will get a great little story or quote with which I may begin my presentation! By doing this visiting and greeting, I have established that something special, unusual, and possibly wonderful is going to happen this morning. The word gets around the room very quickly. I am very careful to visit all the sections of the room. I actually divide the room into eight sections or more. The left and right sections I divide into four quadrants, and then I make sure I've visited and met someone in each of those sections before the conference begins. It's tiring. I have to move very quickly. When I first began doing this about 20 years ago, I could only do one or two of these before time was up and the introductions were beginning. Now I've had so much practice, I can zoom through the room and still relate to each group personally.

I visit with the people in the very back two or three rows and the folks sitting near the side doors. Anyone knitting (yes, there are people who come to meetings and knit, do

their homework or grade someone else's, do their nails, read
the paper, and so on) or otherwise engaged in a pastime, I
make sure I shake their hand and introduce myself. That's
how I soften those who are most likely to be resistant to a
motivational message.

My meeting planner signals me. "We're going to start in
five minutes." I go over and turn off the music cassette. I seat
myself where I'm expected to be during the opening cere-
monies or the kickoff welcoming speaker's address. The meeting begins. But, as you see, I've already begun my motivational presentation over an hour ago, as I set up the room
and began setting up the audience to be open to my talk.

The following several pages include the form provided as
a sample of the kinds of things you might want to include in
a room setup suggestion list to send to your meeting planner.
You will, of course, have to revise this to reflect your own
needs and preferences.

Room Setup Suggestions for
Keynote Address by Dr. Hanoch McCarty

MY GOAL: The best presentation ever! I want to help achieve your goals for this presentation with energy, verve, excitement, motivation, commitment. In order to achieve this, the following *suggestions* are provided. These were developed over many years of consulting work and are provided in order to ensure a smooth and successful presentation. If any of these create a problem for you, please call me, and we'll arrange a satisfactory alternative. I've checked off the items that apply.

_____ 1. The best rooms for this presentation will be an auditorium, multipurpose room, or a hotel meeting room. I can also present this address in a room with a flat, level floor and movable chairs rather than an auditorium. A lunchroom or a gymnasium would do fine. If I am in a flat-floored room, please put me on the *long wall* of the room if at all possible. This will improve sight lines and keep each participant closer to me. This can really make a difference not only for me but for any other speaker in that room. See the diagram provided in Figure 6.1.

Figure 6.1

Setup Diagram for Dr. McCarty's Presentation

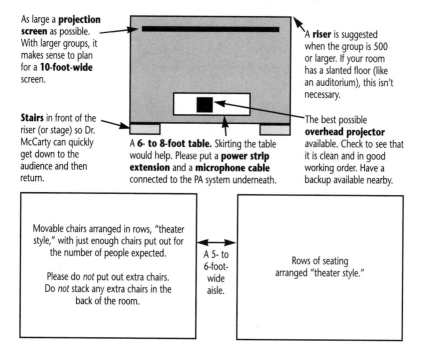

As large a **projection screen** as possible. With larger groups, it makes sense to plan for a **10-foot-wide** screen.

A **riser** is suggested when the group is 500 or larger. If your room has a slanted floor (like an auditorium), this isn't necessary.

Stairs in front of the riser (or stage) so Dr. McCarty can quickly get down to the audience and then return.

A **6- to 8-foot table.** Skirting the table would help. Please put a **power strip extension** and a **microphone cable** connected to the PA system underneath.

The best possible **overhead projector** available. Check to see that it is clean and in good working order. Have a backup available nearby.

Movable chairs arranged in rows, "theater style," with just enough chairs put out for the number of people expected.

Please do *not* put out extra chairs. Do *not* stack any extra chairs in the back of the room.

A 5- to 6-foot-wide aisle.

Rows of seating arranged "theater style."

____ 2. Please check the overhead projector and screen well in advance. It is important that the image be as large as possible so that everyone can clearly see
the transparencies that I use. Make sure that I am not too far from the audience. If I am up on stage or a platform, it will be OK as long as the distance
to the front row is not excessive.

   If there is a wide space between the front of the stage and the first row,
it would be best if my table and projector could be put down in that space,
and I will work from that area, down on the floor with the people. This will
only be practical if the projector can focus on the screen from that distance.
Please check this out and let me know as soon as possible.

____ 3. I would appreciate there being no one on the stage, podium, or dais behind
me during my talk.

____ 4. I need a really good *clear* PA system. I will provide a wireless microphone
system that will plug into your PA. It usually pays (for large groups) to rent
a professional PA system if you aren't absolutely certain about the clarity of
the one available in the auditorium or meeting room. Professional systems
make a surprising quality difference in speech intelligibility.

   I will be bringing with me audio equipment that must be connected to
your PA system. Please help me by having the A/V person available when I
arrive. You can have that person call my office to discuss the setup in
advance at (209) 745-2212 (Pacific coast time).

____ 5. I will need an excellent *bright* overhead projector and a *big* screen. (For
groups larger than about 300, it can really help to rent a professional overhead projector [sometimes called a projector with a "hot burn" or metal
halide bulb] from a local audio-visual company. Professional projectors are
very much brighter, clearer, and more reliable than the ones available in
schools and hotels). And, if possible, a spare projector should be situated
nearby in case of bulb blowout. (This *does* happen at the least convenient
times!)

   If it is possible for you to *focus spotlights* on the front of the area in which
I will be standing when I present, that would add greatly to the effectiveness of the presentation. Please make sure that the spotlights are on the
floor in front of my table and do not spill over onto the projection screen.

____ 6. Please provide a pitcher with ice (not ice water) and some cold noncaf-
feinated soft drinks. I can get very dry when I am doing one of these presentations!

____ 7. If you are in an area where smoking is permitted in public places, please put
up "No Smoking" signs. My experience tells me that fewer than 25 percent
of the audience smokes. The other 75 percent really suffer and are quite
happy when smoking is gently but actively discouraged. If we are in a hotel
meeting room, please make sure ashtrays are *not* put out on the chairs or
tables. The hotel staff may do this automatically unless you specifically ask
them not to.

___ 8. Block off the back rows of the auditorium, leaving only the number of seats equal to the size of the expected group. Assign ushers to place ropes, signs, tape, etc., and to encourage people to respect the ropes and not pull them down or climb over them. *This is very important. A compact group responds better; has better interaction; receives and retains the speaker's message better.*

___ 9. Put out chairs only for the best estimate of the size of the expected group. Have ushers assigned to encourage the people to be seated on time. For some reason, certain people like to stand at the back of the room and talk, smoke, drink coffee. This proves to be extremely distracting to the other participants.

Custodial personnel seem to like to put out many more chairs than are indicated. Please make sure that they don't do this. And, if stacks of extra chairs ("just in case") are to be left out, have them put at the front of the room, *not* at the back! If they are at the back, people will take these chairs rather than sit up front. That will leave the room with six empty rows of chairs at the front and a messy jumble of chairs at the back blocking the exits and fire lanes.

___ 10. I need to know who will pick me up in the morning at the hotel (assuming that I am coming in the night before the presentation), and his or her phone number. This person needs to know that *I must be at the presentation site at least one hour prior to the presentation in order to set up.* It would help if I could have a look at the presentation site the night before in order to discuss last-minute details and to facilitate my planning.

___ 11. Please let me know when I arrive (or before) if there are important issues occurring in the group that may affect their receptivity (i.e., salary negotiations, recent death of a staff member, or the like).

___ 12. For the introduction to my presentation, please use the information supplied on the introduction sheet enclosed. Please have my introducer speak with me before the presentation to go over the introduction. The introduction sheet is provided only as a guideline. If you or your introducer would rather write your own introduction, please feel free to do so.

___ 13. Have your airport pickup person carry a large index card with your group's name written in felt-tip marker. Meet me at the gate or at baggage return.

Flight: _____ Time: _____ Date: _____

___ 14. Have someone designated to return me to the airport immediately after the presentation.

___ 15. Other _____

7 MOTIVATING THROUGH THE POWER OF THE STORY

Everybody is a story. When I was a child, people sat around kitchen tables and told their stories. We don't do that so much anymore. Sitting around the table telling stories is not just a way of passing time. It is the way the wisdom gets passed along. The stuff that helps us live a life worth remembering. Despite the awesome powers of technology many of us still do not live very well. We need to listen to each other's stories once again.

Rachel Naomi Remen, *Kitchen Table Wisdom: Stories That Heal.* York: Riverhead Books, 1996

The best motivational speakers are, really, at the core, story-tellers. Listen to Stephen Covey, and you will hear stories that make his ground-breaking concepts come alive in the minds of his audiences. Listen to Zig Ziglar, and you will be hearing stories that inspire, that bring goosebumps and moments of breakthrough insights. If you've attended a presentation by any well-known public speaker, you've heard that speaker use stories, powerful stories, stories that caught your interest and touched your heart. It is because we all have our own stories that we can relate so well to the stories of others.

Everybody has a story. No matter what we do for a living, how much we have in our bank account, or what the color of our skin may be, we have a story. Each one of us has a story, whether it is visible to the eye or locked inside of us. We are encouraged to believe that our past, our circumstances, both physical and emotional, and our experiences are our story. Our mental picture of our life's story encompasses what we perceive to be true about ourselves and our possibilities.

The life we are born into is not necessarily our destiny. All of us have the power to rewrite our story, to recast the drama of our lives, and redirect the actions of the main character, ourselves. The outcomes of the our lives are determined largely by our responses to each event. Do we choose to be the hero or victim in our life's drama?

There's an old folk tale about twin children who were put into separate rooms. One room was beautifully decorated with many toys and games; the other was a drab room that contained a pitchfork and a mountain of hay. Hours later, the child in the toy room complained of being bored, saying, "I'm tired of this, I want something fun to do." The child in the other room was happily forking hay, quickly and with great intensity. When asked why he was working so hard he replied, "With this much hay, I figure there must be a pony in here somewhere!" Each child had an opportunity to choose his reality, as do all of us when we choose which stories in our lives that we decide to tell.

Good stories, like the best mentors in our lives, are *door openers*. They are unique experiences containing insights tied to emotional triggers that get our attention and stay in our memories. These stories can free us from being bound to decisions of the past and open us to understanding ourselves and the opportunities that are there before us. A really good story allows us to recognize the choices that are open to us and see new alternatives we might never have seen in any other way. It can give us permission to try a new path.

Storytelling is an ancient art. Long before we differenti-
ated job titles like "teacher," or "singer," or "historian," or
"preacher," we had the tribal storyteller, who was often all
those jobs combined into one person. Using dramatic talents,
the storyteller, or later the "troubadour," chanted, sang,
intoned, or simply told the history and the myths, the accumulated wisdom of the tribe. All listened, not just the children. The adults listened because it helped them remember
and comforted them in times of crisis. Some of the stories
involved their own exploits, tales of battles they fought,
places they visited, or difficult winters they survived. It
helped their self-esteem, established or reestablished their
place in the tribe. We get the phrase "unsung hero" from the
Norse custom of singing the hero's exploits upon return from
battle. If someone did not return from the battle, or worse
yet, if no one who witnessed the hero's exploits returned
from that battle, then his bravery couldn't be celebrated and
perhaps he would not be allowed to enter Valhalla.

The story conveyed the group's values, history, and sense
of purpose and often contained actual or idealized advice
about how to cope with life's difficulties and challenges.

How did stories function in your family? Wasn't it almost
precisely the same way? At my family table, my father told us
of his day and my mother encouraged him to tell his story.
Because he was a New York City captain of detectives, his stories were fascinating, sometimes even gory or frightening.
Talking about his day, seemed to be almost therapeutic to
him. And then he'd look up and see his children looking at
him with glowing eyes—that didn't hurt him either.

Then my mother would tell about her day at work. She'd
get very animated and dramatic in her narration. She'd tell
the jokes she heard that day. She'd share the victories and
defeats, the tales of the sales force and the constant flux of
winners and losers at the monthly sales meetings. She, too,

would look around the table to see an admiring audience. We learned, my brother and I, our family values from each of those stories. We didn't call it storytelling, we called it dinner. But televisions had not yet taken over dinner time then. Families were still listening to each other. Only after dinner did we retire to the living room where the TV set could be found. Those dinners were an essential part of my upbringing—and only all these years later did I become aware of it—an equally essential part of my preparation to be a public speaker! My mother's dramatic flourishes and unconscious skill at nonverbal communication were my primer on public speaking, on great teaching.

My parents' use of the story to teach was often deliberate. If I or my brother committed some infraction of the rules or failed to meet their expectations, we could be sure we'd hear an admonitory object lesson story, a tale in which someone "just like us" got in terrible trouble for doing a similar thing. I remember that my grandfather, my mother's dad, was also a dramatic storyteller. My dad was not one of those parents who always told stories romanticizing how great his behavior was as a teen. No, he'd often tell us a story in which he revealed major errors he made or really questionable decisions he had taken then. And these gave him the opportunity to criticize himself as a way of letting us know that we, too, were making some questionable choice. In the process, both of my parents enriched my life, communicated with us and with each other, and passed on family traditions, beliefs, values, and skills. Those skills are often not learned in school but at the family table instead.

Years later, I had become a high school teacher. Apparently I was not too bad at teaching, and my new supervisor called me a "natural-born teacher." At first I was flattered and, I admit, a bit puffed up by such feedback in the second year of my professional experience, but soon I realized that the credit was clearly owed to my parents—any storytelling talent of mine had been modeled and nurtured by them my whole life. If you want to be a storyteller or use great stories in the service of your motivational speeches, go back to your origins. Seek the storyteller of your youth and revisit him or her in person or, at the least, in memory. If you made any family movies or videos of that person, watch them again and again, and see what treasures are there to be mined. If that person is still in your life, audio- or videotape them *now!* Don't waste a moment! The natural storyteller that most families have is an inestimably valuable resource of technique, great stories, and continual modeling of best practice.

THE POWER OF THE STORY

In 1993 a book was published that would eventually make publishing history. The brainchild of noted public speakers and trainers Jack Canfield and Mark Victor Hansen, *Chicken Soup for the Soul* was a collection of one hundred and one stories selected, as the subtitle proclaims, "to open the heart and rekindle the soul."

Canfield and Hansen had developed this concept—that Americans were getting fed up with all the negativity in the news and with the constant cynicism and negative expectation that seemed to mark the 1980s. They believed that people wanted hope. Just as chicken soup is what your Mom would give you when your body wasn't feeling good, they thought that beautiful stories could be "chicken soup for the soul" and help us feel better spiritually. They set out to find stories that would deal with all of life's toughest and most important moments and events: life, death, parenting, loving and caring, and so on. They specifically sought stories that would offer meaning—people would have real problems and confront them, but they would somehow find sense and purpose and personal worth amid their difficulties. Toward that end, they

contacted many members of the National Speakers Association
and Toastmasters International who were their friends, colleagues, or acquaintances. They called and wrote to thousands
of speakers as well as contacting clergy, both famous and
unknown, and great teachers, counselors, and writers. They
asked each, "Do you have a favorite story? Or a story that you
just love to tell at one of your speeches or seminars? The 'killer'
story—the one that absolutely clinches the point you're trying
to make? The story that leaves the audience with tears in their
eyes or convulsed with laughter. That's the kind of story we
want." They described the project they planned and many of
their correspondents sent in stories. I sent in six, myself. They
didn't stop there. They'd already written down all of their own
favorites from their professional work. They read every book,
magazine, journal, or newsletter they could get their hands on,
scouring them for stories with a punch. Slowly, the stories
began to trickle in. Later, the flow increased. So many were
excellent stories, but they had to make sure to eliminate too
much similarity. They were concerned that some stories might
only appeal to them or to the kinds of audiences they usually
addressed and might be less useful or attractive to a wider audience, so they set up a national reader panel of "just plain
folks" all over the United States and Canada. People of every
ethnicity, racial group, gender, age level, and socioeconomic
background were added to the mix. These volunteers were
asked to read every story and rate it on a one-to-ten scale
according to criteria like these:

1. The story has to be short. People are busier than ever.
    They want something that can be read in a short time,
    perhaps just before bedtime or in one visit to the john!
2. The story has to be true. People want inspiration that
    comes from real-life experience.
3. The story has to produce a physiological reaction in the
    reader: laughter, tears, goosebumps, weak knees, a sharp
    intake of breath followed by "Wow!" or "Aha!"

4. The story has to be positive—at least in its final meaning. Even if someone is contending with catastrophe, they've got to find some meaning or hope in the experience.
5. The story has to stand on its own without a moral all neatly stated at the end. We trust our readers to get the point. We don't want preachy stories, just uplifting ones.

When the book was done, it was submitted to a long series of publishers (more than 38), all of whom turned the book down almost immediately. "Not tough enough. Who'd want to read such positive stuff? We've got to swim with the sharks nowadays." Finally, a publisher in South Florida, Health Communications, Inc., agreed to publish the book. The advertising budget was small, but Hansen and Canfield were totally committed to getting the word out about this book. They spent nearly a full year doing almost nothing but promoting the book in every way they could imagine. They asked for help from a startling array of talented people—help in brainstorming marketing methods and help in getting people to read their book.

Little by little, the word did get out. Word-of-mouth takes time but, when it does build, it is a potent force indeed. The book hit the *New York Times* best-seller list and stayed there for over 140 weeks, sometimes number one, sometimes down to number four. It sold well over one million copies in its first year, 1993. As of this writing, in 1998, it has sold over *14 million copies!* The first book had a page at the back called "More Chicken Soup," which explained how to send in your own story. Readers responded in droves and torrents. Now they are receiving between 50 and 200 stories every day at the "Chicken Soup" offices. So they produced another volume, *A 2nd Helping of Chicken Soup for the Soul,* which immediately hit the best-seller lists. The following year, the next volume, *A 3rd Serving of Chicken Soup for the Soul,* was released, and it, too, jumped onto the best-seller charts.

My wife Meladee and I were invited to coauthor the next book in the series. We spent 13 months reading over 4,200 stories, carefully choosing the best ones and then sending copies of them to over 300 readers around the country. We had selected stories from the mounds that had been sent us by mail and by e-mail and that were handed to us by readers and friends. We haunted libraries; we searched the Internet; we contacted storytelling associations and well-known writers. We wrote to famous people, and we read lots of newspaper columns and feature stories, combing, searching, winnowing, and finding many wonderful new stories. We wrote many stories ourselves, gleaned from our life experiences or told to us by acquaintances. All of these went to that reader panel until we had narrowed them down to the 101 absolutely best stories we could find. That volume, *A 4th Course of Chicken Soup for the Soul,* was released in April 1997 and has sold over *1.5 million* copies to date!

At the same time, Jack and Mark Victor were inviting other coauthors to produce spin-off books such as *Chicken Soup for the Woman's Soul, Chicken Soup for the Teenage Soul,* and *Chicken Soup for the Soul at Work.* These, too, became runaway best-sellers in their own right. In fact the whole series has sold in excess of *30 million copies!* I share this story with you not to brag about my own personal success or my friends' but to illustrate to you the incredible power and attraction of stories, well-chosen and affecting stories. There seems to be a nearly insatiable appetite for such stories, and our mail reflects it. We are getting a deluge of mail from readers from all over the world: Kuala Lumpur, Manila, Prague, Warsaw, Seoul, Hong Kong, Jakarta, Jerusalem, as well as all over the United States, Canada, and South America.

Our readers tell us how the stories help them. Many write about the solace such stories provide in moments of life crisis, such as a death in the family or a major illness. Others tell us that they use the stories in their work or in their family lives. Parents tell us they turn off the TV set and read a story or two for an hour each evening. And that reminds them to tell some of their own family stories that they had forgotten to tell in the rush of work and cooking and then dropping gratefully in front of the television. Coaches tell us they use the stories to motivate the team during half-time. Clergy tell us, in large numbers, that these stories have enlivened many a sermon or wedding ceremony and, of course, provided just the right touch at a funeral eulogy. Sales managers write us about how effective it is to use such stories at the sales meeting. In fact, there have been several featured stories in publications like *The Wall Street Journal* and *The Christian Science Monitor* about the spontaneous formation of "Chicken Soup for the Soul™ Groups" at Fortune 500 companies where employees bring a book and a brown-bag lunch one day a week and share stories with colleagues—and their teamwork improves perceptibly! Students write us about their teachers reading one story to start the day and how it helps their attitude about school.

Let us not forget the origins of the very first book: professional speakers, NSA members, who generously shared their stories with Jack Canfield and Mark Victor Hansen. Many, many speakers have written in to thank them for providing "just the right story" to enhance a presentation they were planning. The books have become a major resource for speakers everywhere, and I certainly recommend them to you for that purpose.

HOW A STORY WORKS

Stories can take a good talk and elevate it to a memorable experience. In order to motivate, the speaker must connect with more than the minds of the audience members; he or she has to connect with their hearts, with their core values, and with their most significant experiences and memories. To do this, the speaker must first penetrate beyond the natural reserve, skepticism, defensiveness, or distance that may exist in the audience. Some speakers begin their talks with a personal story, such as something about the process of getting to the meeting (the scary or missed flight, getting lost in the maze of streets in their town, or the like), or a story about their family, or a story about their previous history with this group or a member of it. Having done interviews with a number of the program participants prior to the conference, I am in a unique position of usually having several very good stories about people present in the room, and I find that such stories bring me closer to the audience.

Another approach is to begin with a story that is on the main theme of the speech you are about to give. The story need not be very long nor need it be serious. It can be humorous or tender, serious or light-hearted, but it should definitely be personal, homely, and authentic. As you tell this story, watch the audience. If the story is well chosen, you'll actually see them relax. "Ah, a story, I can relate to that. I can understand that. This presentation won't be one of those boring ones, and it won't be filled with jargon and nit-picking details that put me to sleep. The person on the stage seems real to me." By starting with a good story, you've reassured your audience that you are approachable, a real person, and we learn best from people like ourselves.

I've seen excellent speakers begin with a humorous self-deprecating story, one chosen to deliberately lower their "psychological size," the aura that audiences invest keynote speakers with. By puncturing that balloon, they make it much easier for the audience to see themselves as connected to the ideas that are being presented.

ANCHORING

Stories work by connecting ideas with feelings. If you simply mention important concepts to a group, they may recognize their importance, but few will remember these points because they seem to the listener to be intellectual, cold, and distant. You've offered them no personal reason to remember these ideas. Wrap those same ideas in an affecting story, and no one will forget the story or the ideas associated with them. The story anchors the concepts. Give me an idea, a fact, or a concept while you have me laughing or while you've brought a tear to my eyes, and I will never lose your lesson.

I was presenting a keynote address to a group of 1,500 teachers in Los Angeles. The talk was entitled "You Make THE Difference!" and the goal was to remind them of the unique and awesome power that a really good, truly committed teacher can make in the lives of children. There were a number of key concepts leading to the penultimate one: The time for commitment is right now, that you have to behave every day as though this were your last best opportunity to make the difference in your job. At that moment, I told this true story from my own life.

I was a single parent with full custody of my two little children. Living in Cleveland, I had to fly to Detroit where I was to present a workshop on stress management. The children's nanny was to arrive early that frozen February morning as I was ready to leave for the airport. It was early in my single parenthood, and I had a considerable amount of stress myself in juggling my professorial job, my consulting, my housekeeping, and my parenting. Racing that morning to get ready and to get the children up and dressed and fed, I was overwhelmed with the weight of my responsibilities. Suddenly, I noticed how totally messy my children's room was, and I just lost it. As they say, I went ballistic. I ranted and raved and shouted: "How many times have I told you . . . "

and more preaching. By the time I was ready to leave the house, I had reduced both little children to tears. "Now, kiss Daddy good-bye," I said, my guilt warring with my anger. And then I left for the airport. I drove through gray skies and slushy, icy streets, arrived at the airport, parked, and checked in for the flight.

The plane was an old one, a DC-9, and we strapped ourselves in and took off into an ice storm. As we reached 11,000 feet, the plane leveled off, and the flight attendant began serving soft drinks from a tray she carried down the aisle. Suddenly there was a loud bang, and a hatch (which we could not see) blew off the plane! All the air in the plane whooshed down the fuselage toward that hatch. The flight attendant, startled, threw her tray of Cokes up in the air, and it drenched some of us. She screamed. Then she ran down the aisle toward the cockpit door, which was jammed and bent from the force of the air column that had rushed out of the pressurized plane.

The oxygen masks fell down from their little hatches above us. Very few people had the presence of mind to put them on. A 70-year-old man, sitting one row behind me, had just recovered from triple-bypass heart surgery at the Cleveland Clinic. He was an immigrant from Eastern Europe, and we had talked while waiting in the line to board the plane. He began shouting in a thick accent, "For dis God saved me? For dis God saved me?"

The plane shuddered and began a twisting, shaking rapid descent down toward frozen Lake Erie below us. I looked out the window and realized that I was about to die. At that moment, I did not have my entire life flash before me. Instead only one image came to mind: the picture of my two little ones, standing tearfully facing me, as I yelled at them for their messy room. I realized that my children would forever carry only one last memory of their father—a mental picture of me, red-faced and screaming.

I began to pray, "Dear Lord, if I survive this, if you save us from this crash, I swear I will never again leave the house this way. I will never leave my children in this way again." I am sure that most of the other people on that plane were praying, too. Whether it was the power of our prayers or something else, suddenly the plane leveled off and turned back toward Cleveland. We landed safely and a spontaneous and protracted cheer arose from all of the passengers. Most of us hugged the pilot and copilot as we exited.

And then, paradoxical as it may seem, we all boarded an identical plane and flew to Detroit! When I returned the next evening, I resolved to keep my promise. Every time I left the house after that, I would call my children to me and say, "I want you to know that I love you. I have always loved you. I know that sometimes you may do something that I don't like, or I may be angry at you, but even then I love you. I will always love you." And I would kiss and hug them both. They were charmed by this, our newest family custom. I did it for years.

After a while, when the children had entered adolescence, they would get bored with the ritual and roll their eyes and sigh when I did it. They would even mimic me in a sarcastic tone, "I know you really love us and . . ." But I was determined to keep that commitment. One day, in a great hurry, I forgot to do the little speech and the hugs. Halfway to the airport, my cell-phone rang. It was my daughter, Shayna. "Dad, you forgot to say it and hug us." Enough said, she hung up. I turned my car around and drove home. Using the cell-phone, I called my travel agent and arranged for a later flight. And there were both children, standing by the door looking a bit sheepish to admit that they really loved our ceremony. We cried a bit as we hugged each other. I think that was one of my best days on this planet.

At the end of that story, the audience was teary-eyed. Tissues were everywhere, dabbing at eyes and sniffling was heard in the room. I clinched my point. "You see, no one knows how long God has wound his clock for. We always think we're going to have another day, another week, another year. But who knows? Shall I teach conventionally, conservatively, holding myself back, keeping my fullest commitment in reserve for emergencies? Shall I? No! This is *it!* This is our chance to teach our best lesson, to reach out to that unreachable child just one more time. You make *the* difference! And, in fact, *only you* can make the difference!" I stopped, silent. The audience looked stunned and then erupted with the biggest standing ovation I had then ever received. That is the power of a story to take your ideas and impress them upon someone's heart. That speech was given over seven years ago. I have received more mail and for a longer period of time from members of that audience than from any other group. People not only got the message, they went back to their schools and shared it with others. Many people were told that story by people who were in that room. One told her minister, and he used it in a sermon and then wrote to me. Another woman wrote me that I was sent to her because she had been so burnt out as a teacher and was no longer "alive to the kids," as she put it. That speech, but most importantly, that story, offered her the path back to rediscovering her own energy and spirit in her job. That's the power of the story as a door-opener.

IDEAS AND FEELINGS

America was formed in the 18th century, the Age of Reason. We have a long-standing bias toward thinking that every problem can be solved with enough effort, thought, energy, time, or money. If I want to convince someone of something,

I should therefore marshal good, logical reasons, proofs, scientific information, and inundate them with it. In actual practice, such a strategy seems to alienate most listeners, leave them cold, unmoved, and unconvinced, or even puts them to sleep.

Are we motivated by logic or by our feelings and needs? Try this experiment: Find out the actual odds of winning your state's lottery—the grand prize. One phone call to the lottery commission will usually produce this information. The odds are astronomically against your actually winning. Ask a mathematician to explain whether or not you affect your odds by purchasing 10, 20, or even 100 tickets. The answer may surprise you. Now, the next time you speak to a large group, give them that information, and ask them if it will affect their decision to buy or not buy a lottery ticket. Now, do a little more research—the Internet is great for this—and find some of the follow-up studies done on former lottery winners—how many had heart attacks or strokes, how many had marital problems apparently brought on by or exacerbated by being a big winner. Read some of the interviews with big winners about the changes in their lives—the long-lost relatives who suddenly surfaced wanting a share; the fear of their children being kidnapped; the fact that their liability increases because of their so-called "deep pockets," causing them to have to radically increase all their insurance policy limits; their need for unlisted phones; and so on. Now give that information to your large audience, and ask them if it would prevent them from buying a ticket or wanting to win. The answer? I've conducted this experiment many times. It's always the same: No one changes. They all want to win. Those who buy tickets will keep on buying tickets. "Oh, that's what happened to *them*. It wouldn't happen to *me!* I could handle it. Anyway, it's fun to dream, isn't it?"

Logic disappears when emotions are high, when need is great. The unique power of the story is that it taps in to that pool of emotion that lies just beneath the cool façade of rationality that many people affect. We must use logic, and we must offer ideas, facts, studies, proofs, and all that, but they will not work to motivate an audience without adding the appropriate emotional core that comes with an appropriate story.

HOW TO FIND YOUR STORIES

Most of the best stories you will ever find to use in your motivational speeches will come from your own life experience. Having said that, I am aware of how tempting it is to see one's own life as prosaic, dull, and having few dramatic stories that might interest an audience. It is precisely because most of one's own stories come from an ordinary life that the audiences will be able to relate to them.

Here are some possible places to find your own personal stories. Think about the first job you ever had. Anything interesting happen then? Anything embarrassing? Did you learn anything that you've used ever since?

Think of other firsts in your life: your first date, the first time you were fired from a job (if ever), the first traffic ticket you received, your first car, your first year at college, and so on. Firsts have a way of being dramatic, at least in our memories. Intense experiences can also be the source of important things we've learned and can share.

Are you a parent? If you were telling me about one of your children, what stories about that child would you tell? Would some be funny? Would others bring a tear to my eyes?

There are life cycle changes that stir deep emotions and are the source of much potential insight in our lives: marriage, births, death, the onset of religious faith. Each of these areas is likely to have more than one useful story from your own experience.

In Creative Writing 101, the teacher tells us that a good story should have "tension, then resolution." The main character ought to change, learn, or grow, or tragically fail to learn or grow from an experience. The tension can come from the character's struggles, striving, or stress. Apply those same rules to your search for personal stories: When you were struggling to learn something, to get a job, to find love, and so on, what occurred, and how did it change you? What new insights or perceptions did you acquire and what caused them?

Sigmund Freud wrote about "the amnesia of childhood," saying that we all have very selective memories about our youth. To find more personal stories, ask your parents, your aunts and uncles, siblings, and friends who knew you then. You'll be surprised at what you'll learn about yourself. Many great stories can be found this way.

OTHER PEOPLE'S STORIES

As a professional speaker, many of my stories are gleaned from my clients and/or their employees. During the interviews that I conduct, I am always alert for a good story. If I laugh when I hear a story related to me, then my audience will laugh, too. If I am touched or impressed, so will they be. My interviewing doesn't stop when I've prepared the speech. On the way to the presentation—on the plane, in the taxi, when I am being picked up by the meeting planner, I am always conducting interviews. I try to turn the conversation away from myself and back to the other person. There's an old saying attributed to Confucius: *"Man was born with two ears and one mouth—it must be a message from God."* I believe that by consciously reminding myself to be a listener, I have enabled myself to find the best stories.

Take Notes All the Time

Don't trust your memory. Carry a small notebook or a pack of 3 x 5 index cards or something on which to take notes. Make it your habit to never be without it. Those little stories you are told by your meeting planner or by a program participant you meet while checking in to the hotel are golden. And the genius, the special spirit of the story is in the details you may forget overnight. While working the crowd prior to the talk, I am listening, listening, asking good questions, and listening. When I hear something usable, I quickly jot key words or phrases and the person's name along with facts like their job title and the unit or division where they work, or I'll ask for their business card. I have found stories to be so powerful and evocative that I even keep little notepads in my car, on my bedside nightstand, anywhere I might have an idea or an insight or be reminded of a story.

I was invited to do a keynote address followed by a half-day seminar for a suburban school district in the Southwest. They invited me to come a day earlier and attend their retreat up in the mountains, and I accepted. It would be a unique chance to see the beautiful scenery and experience this part of the Southwest and a great opportunity to meet the people with whom I'd be working. This group really knew how to chow down! They had a good old-fashioned barbecue out under the pine trees at the edge of a mountain meadow. Rough-hewn log picnic tables surrounded the cook fire, and we were to stay in cabins that looked like old line shacks. It was really roughing it, Western style. There was a lot of good-natured bantering and lots of cold beer and sizzling steaks. People loosened up and spoke with me about how much they loved living and working in that area. And then, a bit sheepishly, most would say something about how they loved working with their colleagues in this school district. Many approached me to tell stories validating someone else's kindness to others or their going far out of their way to help some colleague who was ill or struggling.

The next morning, I made my way around the group, visiting from table to table at breakfast, asking permission to use some of the stories I had been told. I had prepared a very good keynote address but now, with their help, I believed I had a great one.

Ask Good Questions

Get past the basic facts, "And what is your job title?" or, "How long have you worked for the company?" These are closed-ended questions and only lead to very short, often monosyllabic answers. Move toward questions like "What are the three best things about your job?" "What advice would you give a new hire?" "What are you most proud of in the way you've done your job in the past few years?" "If you had a magic wand and could change three or four things here, what would they be?" "What's the funniest thing that's happened to you at work?" "What do you think are the two secret reasons for your company's great success?" These are open-ended questions that invite creativity and allow for unusual, often surprising answers. I've even used, "Tell me a story about your job and the way you do it." The answers you'll get with open-ended questions are very often the gem-like quotes and short stories that bring a sense of immediacy, relevance, and reality to your speech. People will know you've been there on the firing line with them when you've asked such questions and have front-line stories to tell.

Asking Permission

Having gleaned stories from program participants, employees, and others, make sure to ask permission before you use them.

The last thing you want is to be seen as having violated someone's confidences or having deliberately embarrassed someone—especially when you were trying to celebrate them. Ask permission, and let them know where you're going to use the story—in your presentation to the whole group or in some publication. If you will be publishing it, get written permission, or don't use the story!

USING THE STORY

There are three places to use a story in a motivational address. The first is at the very beginning to create a relationship between you and the audience. Of course the introducer helped you by establishing your background and your expertise. It was the beginning of your achieving credibility in the eyes of your audience. Your first few minutes further builds that credibility as the audience members size you up, evaluate your style, and decide where to place you in their value system. Somewhere in the first five minutes, tell that personal story, that humble incident or insight that will establish you as a real person in their eyes.

The second place is using the story to clinch a point, to make a concept come alive or become concrete for the audience. Statistics don't mean anything until you understand them one person at a time. You are speaking about the Holocaust. You rattle off a litany of figures, six million dead, this many death camps, that much money and property stolen, and so on. After a while, your audience's minds shut down. Bring in one Holocaust survivor, and introduce that person. Ask him or her to speak about his or her own family, losses, pain, and the audience is transfixed, stunned, unable to look away. The Holocaust has become real, and Hitler's monstrousness is made plain in ways that huge mountains of evidence based on just statistics can never do.

The company has a wonderful community service program. They've helped 3,500 aged people, served 120,000
meals, read stories in 24 elementary schools to 12,000 children, and on and on. The numbers are impressive but
soporific. However, tell a story about one elementary school
classroom and how one company employee, on released
time, made a huge difference for the children in one fourth-
grade classroom, and the program has just become something
to be proud of.

More than one story can be told in the body of your talk.
In fact, you can illustrate and enhance each major point you
make using a short dramatic story. The danger is too many,
too long. Your impact will be blunted if you overdo storytelling. Pick them for maximum impact, and try, if possible,
to have them congruent in tone and theme, because that will
help glue your talk together into one comprehensible whole.
Perhaps end each story with a repeating phrase. "Another
Cooper Corporation success!" or "Did he give up? Never!"
The rolling rhythm of that phrase punctuating the end of
each story will help tie them all together.

The final use of a story is in your ending. It is where you
use your "killer" story—the story that you have that will
absolutely touch every heart. It's the story that sums up the
whole talk because it speaks to the major theme underlying
your words. Suddenly it all comes together. The story inte-
grates the many elements of your speech. Here is where you
pull out all the stops. The audience will not mind if you are
corny, sentimental, or even the dreaded "touchy-feely," if
your story is well-chosen and delivered with your own passion clearly showing.

This is not the time to hold back. This is not the moment
for you to be laid-back, cool, professional, uninvolved, objec-
tive. You are finally at the moment that you want to let it all
out and give of yourself unashamedly. Your audience really

wants you to do this. Most of them would be too embarrassed to say the things you're going to say. Most really love their jobs and love their professions. They want to be motivated, they want to be able to say, "Gosh, I really love this job! I look forward to coming here and I love working with my team." However, at this end of the century moment, there's been too much cynicism, sarcasm, and negativity for them to be able to say these things out loud. It would be uncool to say them. It wouldn't be uncool for you to say them, though, and by doing so, allow them to agree with you through applause. If the audience members at a motivational keynote address were able to articulate it, they'd beg you to be fully engaged at this moment. In some African-American churches, where call-and-response is the style, you hear it out loud. The speaker, whether preacher or not, says something impassioned, and many call out, "Amen!" "Tell it like it is!" "Glory!" This is not a moment for theory or for intellectualization, it is the moment for passionate commitment. Shout your story—or parts of it. Sing your story if you can. Move your story because you are moving dynamically as you tell it and because you are moved by it—and the audience will gratefully be close behind.

SPEAKING FROM YOUR HEART

Intentionality

SPEAKING IS A *PERFORMING* ART!

It's not only the words. No speech can be thought of as simply the words written or the words delivered to the audience, although the words are very important. Word choice is not a random event—each word conveys its denotative or dictionary meaning and its connotative or associative meaning. And the context of the words as they fit together creates another meaning that may be conveyed to the audience. You've crafted those words: agonized over them, rewritten, redrafted, read your speech aloud, and changed your mind on this section or that. Then you went back to the text and edited again. And now you have that talk, and it's ready to present. If you get up and simply read the speech, no matter how well crafted it may be, it cannot be the effective motivational speech you want it to be without paying attention to the delivery process: *How* was it presented?

"It ain't watcha do, it's the way thatcha do it!"

This was the title of a Benny Goodman song of the 1940s. The words alone do not and cannot convey your full meaning nor accomplish your deeper purpose. The words alone can convey much meaning—as they must do if you send a written document to someone. If your purpose is to inform, you can probably accomplish a great deal of your goal by just these words you've chosen. If, however, your purpose is to motivate, to turn people on, to light their fire, or to make it possible for them to believe again, you must offer those words to them in a dramatic way. As Marshall McLuhan said, "The medium is the message." Your medium is yourself, your body, hands and arms, your face and its expression, your voice, tone, breathing. You become your message. Everything about you that the audience can perceive is melded together with your words. You cannot divorce them. A statement made by Mother Teresa, "We must love everyone—even the least of us," would become a totally different one if those words had been spoken by Saddam Hussein. Who you are is a powerful statement that colors the way your words are received. How you conduct yourself, how you dress and move, how loudly or softly you speak are elements that alter what your audience gleans from your talk.

Verbal: Your Word Choice

Words are not usually chosen by accident. Sigmund Freud, in describing what we now call a "Freudian slip," taught us that there may be a purpose or meaning of which we are not fully conscious, in choosing certain things to say. You are aware of wanting to talk about the problem of overweight, but you find yourself using words like tubby, chunky, fatso, and flabby. Most people would find those words to be negative and judgmental. You could have said overweight, healthy-looking, or plump, which most people would find less negative or offensive. Did you choose the words knowingly? Even if you did not, your listeners will conclude something about you or your message from those choices.

Similarly, as you prepare a motivational talk, it is smart to discover the words that have the most positive and negative meaning to your audience. What are their buzzwords, and are those words appropriate to use with them? What jargon terms ought you use, and which should you avoid? Do they have a history with certain words? For example, while I was a professor at Cleveland State University in the College of Education, we had a dean who encouraged us to form "task forces" to solve certain problems. It was a word appropriated from the Navy and conveyed a serious purpose, an almost militarily disciplined approach to confronting a problem and obliterating it. The use of "task force" would have been excellent except: (1) the problems were defined by the dean, not by the faculty, so there wasn't very much commitment on our part to dealing with them; (2) the task forces were seen as extra committee assignments given to people whose schedules were already overloaded; and, most damning of all, (3) the conclusions and reports by the task forces were rarely, if ever, acted upon. We ended up spending several years working on these task forces and seeing almost nothing come of that investment of our time and energy. A few years later, another new dean arrived. When he announced that he was going to create *task forces* to define our mission, there was a collective groan. He should have checked this out before becoming public with that idea. Many people immediately lumped him together, in their minds, with that previous dean and stopped listening.

Connotative versus Denotative

Words have dictionary meanings, which are the general, agreed-upon definitions that, in the absence of other information, are what we expect them to mean. But words have also acquired associational meanings as well. The history a word has becomes associated with it and colors its meaning even to the point of reversing it. Words that were safe to use in public discourse have become questionable or even dangerous—for instance, many words related to gender such as chair*man*, steward*ess*, fire*man*, referring to women as "girls" or "gals," and so on.

It is not only important to avoid words that may offend audience members' sensitivities for the sake of what has become known as political correctness, it is important because avoiding that is simply kinder and more caring. In addition, unless one is talking directly about the issue of appropriate language or about sexism and/or racism, one ought to avoid these red-flag words because they distract the audience from your main message and mission.

Make every effort to discover what are the red-flag words special to this group. *Down-sizing, out-sourcing, incentive programs,* and *competency-based* are examples of terms that might raise sore feelings in particular groups. Every group has its own dialect or jargon. If you choose to appropriate some of that jargon for use in your speech, make sure you've learned the correct ways to use those words and phrases, or they can backfire and cause a reaction, like laughter, that may be inimical to the point you are making at the time.

Nonverbal: Your Physical Ways of Being as You Say Those Words

For the purposes of our discussion, I define "verbal" as limited to the words you say, in the order in which you say them. The speech you wrote or delivered is the verbal message. Your voice qualities, tone, timbre, pitch, resonance, voice production, breathing, sonority, and so on I characterize as "vocal." Finally, everything else about your speech I assign to the category of "nonverbal."

Nonverbal communication is estimated to carry as much as 93 percent of your message to the audience. The vocal channel is said to carry about 38 percent of the message, and 55 percent is carried by the nonverbal, which includes timing, movement, body posture, gesture, facial expression, and so on. Only about 7 percent of your total message is carried by the words you chose. Most presenters, speech teachers, and other professionals are aware of these estimates and spend a considerable amount of effort in training for improvement of the nonverbal channel of communication.

I believe, from my own experience, that the foregoing is a fairly accurate picture of how communication works. If we have a beautiful speech, filled with well-chosen words and appropriate and affecting stories and can choose to have it delivered in a monotone by a very stiff person who avoids eye contact and seems to be reading it to the audience OR we can choose to have it delivered with drama and gusto by someone who is skilled at integrating nonverbal, vocal, and verbal messages into a seamless and dynamic whole, I am sure that the audience will respond better, much better, to the second version rather than the first. However, if that same excellent address is delivered by an inexperienced speaker whose voice occasionally quavers and whose eye contact is sporadic and whose command of nonverbal is weak or nonexistent but who is authentically committed to the topic and concerned about the audience, the audience will respond enthusiastically to that speaker because the commitment, concern, and caring shine through. They create credibility for the speaker. The audience relates to the speaker, identifies with him or her, and wants the message, too. Conversely, audiences have the ability to smell something wrong when they are being manipulated. The speaker who is a master of delivery but has faked the commitment and simulated the caring will eventually be found out.

Nonverbal is important and can have a great impact on the reception of the message, but the authenticity or credibility of the speaker is even more important. The nonverbal aspect of speaking consists of these ten factors:

1. Posture
2. Carriage
3. Facial expression
4. Gestures
5. Distance or proximity
6. Touch
7. Movement or dynamism
8. Eye contact
9. Timing and pacing
10. Congruence

1. Posture

Your posture does, as your mother probably told you, reveal a lot about you. Do you slump? As you walk out on the stage, what does your posture say to the audience? Do you lean on a podium? Does your body lean forward or backward? All of these are read by your audience as indicators of your interest in them and commitment to your own message.

2. Carriage

How you move and hold yourself is called "carriage." Carry yourself with dignity and energy. Walk upright, stride onto the stage rather than saunter. Some speakers actually bound up onto the stage! I have, however, seen speakers whose slow walk up to the podium conveyed tiredness and lack of their own motivation. Avoid swaying back and forth because that conveys uncertainty as well as distracting the audience from full attentiveness. Plant your feet squarely. Don't put all your weight on one or the other.

3. Facial Expression

Go to a mirror and face it. Close your eyes. Imagine yourself looking very alert, energized, open, and friendly. Make your face reflect that set of feelings. Now open your eyes, and see if the mirror shows what you intend. If it does, your eyebrows will be up somewhat, your eyes will be wide open, and you'll be smiling at least slightly. Practice your facial expression so that you know what you look like when you are feeling the feelings that you want to project to others. Don't pretend to be blasé or unfeeling. Don't pretend you're playing poker. Now is the time to be animated. In an intimate conversation, the other person is usually close enough to see very subtle cues in your facial expression. While speaking to a large group, you must have correspondingly larger expressions so that even those in the back row can have a sense of your animation.

4. Gestures

My mother told me, "Never talk with your hands." In fact, she sometimes made me sit on my hands while I spoke as a way of training me. I want to go on record as valuing most of my mother's lessons, but this one was plainly wrong. People do talk with their hands and speakers, to be understood and believed, absolutely must do so!

I watched the principal of a small town high school speak to a teacher's meeting. All of his gestures were held in close to his body. His elbows were held close to his sides as his hands and forearms made these odd, abortive gestures. His words were about how the faculty had to "get out there and fight, fight, fight for community support on the coming tax levy vote." His gestures had no fight in them. Later, I found that he was, himself, being micromanaged by the school board. It occurred to me that he really didn't feel that he had the room to fight for what he needed, and his gestures mirrored that situation.

As the motivational speaker, you've got to get the attention and interest of the group. Your gestures have to be much larger, more expansive, and communicate your confidence, your sense of decisiveness and authority. Watch any television preacher, and you'll get a fairly good idea of the size and power of gestures appropriate for motivational speaking.

Avoid weak gestures like keeping your hands behind your back or clasped prayerfully as though you were begging for the audience to pay attention. Also avoid "fiddling" gestures like repeated touching of your hair, tapping, or twirling your ring on your finger. Keep your hands out of your pockets. If you have difficulty thinking of what to do with your hands, put something in them—a prop like a laser pointer, the remote control for your laptop or slide projector, or a sample of the products of the company.

5. Distance or Proximity

One way you are communicating nonverbally is through the distance you take or allow between yourself and your audience. Standing behind a podium, for example, takes on the authority of the podium but separates you from your audience and encourages you to be static, unmoving. Standing up on a stage brings you that authority or aura of specialness, but also distances you from the audience. You have to decide which stance makes the most sense with a given group or within the confines of your comfort level. I find that most times I want to be able to leave the stage (or riser) and go down among the people for certain special moments during my talk. I often request that the stairs (which hotel meeting rooms put at the sides of the riser usually) be placed in front to facilitate that. Sometimes, I am in an auditorium or other venue that prevents my going into the audience and, while I cope with this as best I can, it still restricts my connecting with the audience as intimately as my style demands. I wear a wireless microphone and often carry an additional one so I can do my version of Oprah Winfrey and conduct little impromptu interviews with participants as a part of my presentation. I recommend that you play with this distance versus closeness dimension and see how it can work for you.

6. Touch

In most motivational speaking, there are very few opportunities for touch, yet touch is a powerful vehicle for communication. A hug, a handshake, the pat on the back are all examples of touch that builds relationship and closeness. There are, if you construct them, places that touch can be built in to your talk, to great effect. For example, you can shake the hand of your introducer as you approach the podium. You can, as I do, spend time before the beginning of the meeting greeting participants and introducing yourself to them, accompanied by handshakes. If you are courageous and corny enough, you can—as I often do—go out into the audience and connect with participants and reach out to hold someone's hand as you talk to them in front of the group.

In a recent keynote, I had visited the company a month earlier and done my employee interviews. At that time, I took pictures of my interviewees and got stories from them of examples of "going above and beyond the call of duty." One told a story about a coworker who had done an incredibly caring act of kindness for a person in their community and how well this person had represented the values that the company held dear. I went to meet this employee and take a picture of him as well. During my keynote, there was the moment I build in to celebrate "unsung heroes" of the company. I put this individual's picture on the screen (which was a total surprise to him) and called him up to the stage to accept an award. As he came up, I reached out to shake his hand, and he saw it as an invitation to be hugged, so we hugged. The applause was deafening! Touch, when it's appropriate, can be very powerful in making everyone feel connected to you and to your message.

7. Movement or Dynamism

I have seen really excellent speakers who stay behind the podium. One of them, Dr. Samuel Betances, is among the most dynamic speakers I have ever heard. He stays behind the podium almost religiously. Yet his gestures are so large, his face so animated, and his voice so beautifully modulated that his lack of movement is not a drawback. He replaces movement with other dramatic nonverbal information.

Movement away from the podium can be an important element in bringing drama and visual interest to your presentation. There are many professional speakers who rarely, if ever, use a podium. Harry Wong, who is one of the most popular and effective educational speakers in America, nearly flies around the stage. He uses a wireless microphone because he cannot be tied down in one place. He is at stage left and then stage right; he's down in the audience and then back at the projector table. He makes sure that all sides of the audience feel that he is speaking directly to them. Of course, movement is only one of his tools; his animated voice, moving quickly from excited loudness to an intense whisper, grabs and keeps the audience's rapt attention.

Many speakers have unconscious preferences for right or left of the stage and of the audience. They find themselves talking 70 percent to one side of the audience and only 30 percent to the other. Keep in mind that you want to do as Harry Wong does and involve everybody.

Movement includes your entry into the venue and everything else you do until you are home or away from any member of the audience or the committee that brought you in. When I arrive at least an hour to 90 minutes before the talk

and begin my preparations, the committee is very aware of
my movement and whether or not I seem confident, bold, in
command of myself and my material. I don't wander around,
I move purposefully. After I am finished with my preparations, I am involved in doing my audience greeting, my prepresentation interviews, and just plain networking. I am
being observed by my audience. All of this contributes to the
final impression I am making. Where am I just prior to being
introduced? It varies according to the situation. If I have my
preference, I am standing on the side, near the front of the
room. I am not moving then so I do not distract the audience
or the introducer or program chair. I bound up to the podium
as soon as my introducer finishes and shake his or her hand
and leap into my talk. When I am done, my movements and
gestures—facing the audience, stage center—include a very
slight bow, which often cues them into their applause. When
the applause is done, I am walking to a seat—if there's
another presenter upcoming or I am going down into the
audience to meet people who want to speak with me. If I
have product for sale, I do not go to the product table; people
did not come for a commercial event, they came to hear the
talk. I have arranged for someone to work at the table and
sell product so I can give my entire attention to the people
who were gracious enough to listen to me.

As I leave the hall, and as I make my way out of the
building, my movement is still on display. I am careful to
continue to present the same professional persona that I had
in the hall.

8. Eye Contact

My college speech teacher told us to "speak to the very
back of the room." I suppose this is great advice if the person
grading you is sitting there, but it ignores the fact that everyone in front of where you are focusing will feel left out,

ignored, or devalued by you. Mentally divide up the room into sections. I recommend eight or ten sections and then make it your business to make eye contact, in turn, with audience members in each section. Do it randomly so it doesn't look like you're simply sweeping your eyes across the group. Pick out individuals in each section to focus on and then vary those individuals on your next go-around.

I have a strategy to pick the most resistant looking people in each section and deliberately include them in my eye contact. I also pick the person who's smiling at me or seeming the most positive and include him or her as well. The latter group are included because they give me energy. Don't keep going back to the same five people or they will feel singled out, sometimes negatively, even though you are being positive! Keep switching your focus people.

Even if you are reading your talk, try to maintain eye contact with your audience. Type your talk out in readable phrases, and number every fifth line. (Good word processing programs usually have this as a built-in feature.) This will allow you to look down quickly and find your next phrase and then look up at the audience while saying that whole phrase from memory. Then another quick look down and so on.

9. Timing and Pacing

Do you seem rushed? Very often beginning speakers want so very much to please and to succeed, they put way too much material into the talk. There's really enough there for a two-day seminar, not a 45- to 60-minute motivational talk. In an overly packed speech, you will find yourself zooming material toward the end. The end is when you should be doing material in a way that lets the audience savor your words. At the end should be your best material, your sure-fire story whose punch line will sweep the audience of their collective feet. You don't want to rush at that moment. Think of your talk as having from three to five major points. More than this can be tiresome and self-defeating.

Timing also refers to your delivery of punch lines. A punch line is, in a joke, the laugh line, the ending whose surprise generates the laugh. The key line in a story is also the punch line—the ending whose insight, or wisdom, or content resolves the conflict of the story. You need to build to your punch line and then pause before delivering it. Use vocal cues to alert your audience to the imminence of the key line. Get louder or softer, use a gesture that will be unmistakable. There are so many ways—stop, look down, get silent for just five seconds. Then, look up at the audience and spread your arms and deliver your line. Use any sequence of vocal and nonverbal cues that will make it impossible to miss the line. I have seen stories that were absolutely perfect and yet did not work in that talk because the speaker threw away the punch line. It came and went so fast the audience didn't notice it. In fact, many jokes have a lot of repetition in them simply to build the tension that the punch line will resolve and to make it clear when the punch line arrives, because it's the first line that is different. Experiment with timing. Build the tension, pause, and count the beats. This time deliver the punch after four beats, the next time after three. Find what works for you.

10. Congruence

Very few single nonverbal cues are the make-or-break cues that determine the success or failure of your speech. Instead, it is the constellation of cues you send that adds up to the total impression you've made. Are your nonverbal cues congruent? There was a love song in 1911 that had the title, "Your Lips Tell Me No-No, But There's Yes-Yes in Your Eyes!" If you are moving dynamically, your face is animated, your gestures are large and appropriate, your eye contact is maintained, you are sending a congruent message. Nothing is out of place and the audience gets the message: You are prepared, you are confident, you are excited and interested and motivated yourself—and then they can choose to be, too.

THE VOCAL CHANNEL

As I pointed out earlier, communication experts tell us that about 38 or 40 percent of the message that gets communicated comes across on the vocal channel. This includes your tone of voice, pitch, inflection, volume, speed and articulation, breathing, vocal source, and timing.

Your vocal tone, pitch, and inflection can be monotonically flat or musically varied. If it is too varied, you will have a sing-song effect that most American audiences will find annoying. If it is too unvaried, it will be experienced as boring. Audiotape yourself, listen to segments, and give yourself feedback about your vocal tone. This is an area where vocal coaching can lead to big improvements.

Volume is another area where people often get stuck at one setting. Speakers can get in the habit of shouting at their audiences or speaking at such a low volume that even the microphone doesn't pick their voices up well. The important thing is to vary your volume in order to maintain audience interest, to emphasize certain points, and more often, to emphasize certain parts of your sentence. Mark Victor Hansen will begin a sentence at a moderately high volume, indicating his high interest in what he is saying, and then build the volume and the speed at which he is talking and then abruptly stop, pause, and continue in a near whisper. The audience is captivated. The variety and emphasis make the end of that sentence absolutely unforgettable.

Speed and Articulation

How quickly do you speak? There have recently been interesting studies about the relationship of the speaker's perceived power and his or her speed of speaking. The speakers who were seen as younger and less politically or personally powerful were found to be the most rapid speakers, and the older or more powerful speakers were found to be the slowest, who also took long pauses between words. It turns out to be a cue that the audience both helps create and responds to. When the audience knows it will be hearing from a famous person, they seem to become ready to listen and allow the speaker much leeway about how to present. In one study, they taped politicians running for office and measured how long they spoke, how long the pauses were between their words and sentences, and how much of their speeches were actually played on air. Then they did the same study on politicians who had left office. The findings were interesting: The more powerful the politician was seen to be, the more likely the group would let him or her start the talk late (without leaving). The audience members were also more likely to stay until the sometimes bitter end. The excerpts from the incumbent's speech shown on the evening news were longer than those shown when that same politician had been running for office. Slower equates with power in the American mind, at least.

This discussion of the verbal, vocal, and nonverbal channels was not provided for you to *simulate* commitment to your topic. The smooth and skilled but insincere speaker will eventually be found out and dismissed as a phony. But the sincere speaker, wanting to be more effective, needs to work on improving his or her use of those channels. I recommend audio- and videotaping yourself consistently, over time, to help you hone your ability to communicate "on all frequencies." In using taping, don't tape everything and then force yourself to listen to or watch each tape in its entirety. This can be very painful and tedious. Instead, encourage yourself to audit one small segment of perhaps ten minutes from each presentation that you do. Give up rating yourself on some internal scale because most excellent people have a streak of perfectionism that will cause you much pain. Instead, take the position that "there's always something to learn from every presentation." Choose to work on one thing rather than on long lists of deficiencies you may find. Having worked on and improved that one thing, go on to the next, following your own schedule. Be patient with yourself.

Intentionality

All the components of the vocal channels and nonverbal channels can prove to be essential in helping make your motivational speaking successful. No one, however, can be successful at this profession unless they achieve *intentionality*. It's a combination of factors that, when mixed together in the right container, will lead to that most wonderful and rare event, the perfect conference that ends in a great ovation and a very grateful meeting planner. *Intentionality is the speaker's total commitment to and belief in the speech's importance, value, interest, usefulness, and effectiveness.* When a speaker has intentionality, he or she has the intention to succeed, confidence in his or her message and its worth, and the conviction that he or she can get that message across to each and every member of the audience.

The audience reads intentionality as it watches and listens from the very beginning of your preparation or the parts of it they see and hear. How can you motivate someone else if you are not motivated? How can you encourage others to believe in something if you do not believe in it? People can be fooled by very good actors, but as Abe Lincoln said, "You can fool all of the people some of the time and some of the people all of the time . . . " Eventually, the audience does read you, and it does so by reading all those verbal, vocal, and nonverbal channels. Both consciously ("I really like what he's saying," or, "She's got such a sincere tone of voice,") and unconsciously ("I don't know what it is, but there's something I don't trust about that guy. He seems like he's just putting it on. It doesn't all hang together,"), the audience sums up all the information and comes to a conclusion of belief in you and your message— or not. When they do buy in to you and your message, it is because you have demonstrated intentionality.

Your intention is to motivate and to do so in a way respectful of your audience. Your intention is to advocate a position, an attitude, a program, or a new idea, or you were there to reinvigorate a group grown tired and needing a shot in the arm. Having done your homework, you saw the value and worth of the group and its programs, and you bought in yourself. It is your belief and your being convinced that will convince others.

When you find yourself eager to get up to speak, you have intentionality. When you discover in yourself a delight or even a joy in speaking to this group on that topic, you have intentionality. When you allow yourself to let go all stops and put yourself fully into the moment, letting go of worrying about how you look or what others may think, at that moment you are the living embodiment of intentionality, and you cannot fail to motivate this group.

Now, go out there and *give 'em heaven! Knock 'em alive!*

About Toastmasters International

If the thought of public speaking is enough to stop you dead in your tracks, it may have the same effect on your career.

While surveys report that public speaking is one of people's most dreaded fears, the fact remains that the inability to effectively deliver a clear thought in front of others can spell doom for professional progress. The person with strong communication skills has a clear advantage over tongue-tied colleagues—especially in a competitive job market.

Toastmasters International, a nonprofit educational organization, helps people conquer their pre-speech jitters. From one club started in Santa Ana, California, in 1924, the organization now has more than 170,000 members in 8,300 clubs in 62 countries.

How Does It Work?

A Toastmasters club is a "learn by doing" workshop in which men and women hone their communication and leadership skills in a friendly, supportive atmosphere. A typical club has 20 members who meet weekly or biweekly to practice public speaking techniques. Members, who pay approximately $35 in dues twice a year, learn by progressing through a series of 10 speaking assignments and being evaluated on their performance by their fellow club members. When finished with the basic speech manual, members can select from among 14 advanced programs that are geared toward specific career needs. Members also have the opportunity to develop and practice leadership skills by working in the High Performance Leadership Program.

Besides taking turns to deliver prepared speeches and evaluate those of other members, Toastmasters give impromptu talks on assigned topics, usually related to current events. They also develop listening skills, conduct meetings, learn parliamentary procedure and gain leadership experience by serving as club officers. But most importantly, they develop self-confidence from accomplishing what many once thought impossible.

The benefits of Toastmasters' proven and simple learning formula has not been lost on the thousands of corporations that sponsor in-house Toastmasters clubs as cost-efficient means of satisfying their employees' needs for communication training. Toastmasters clubs can be found in the U.S. Senate and the House of Representatives, as well as in a variety of community organizations, prisons, universities, hospitals, military bases, and churches.

How to Get Started

Most cities in North America have several Toastmasters clubs that meet at different times and locations during the week. If you are interested in forming or joining a club, call (714) 858-8255. For a listing of local clubs, call (800) WE-SPEAK, or write Toastmasters International, PO Box 9052, Mission Viejo, California 92690, USA. You can also visit our website at http://www.toastmasters.org.

As the leading organization devoted to teaching public speaking skills, we are devoted to helping you become more effective in your career and daily life.

Terrence J. McCann
Executive Director, Toastmasters International